D1531656

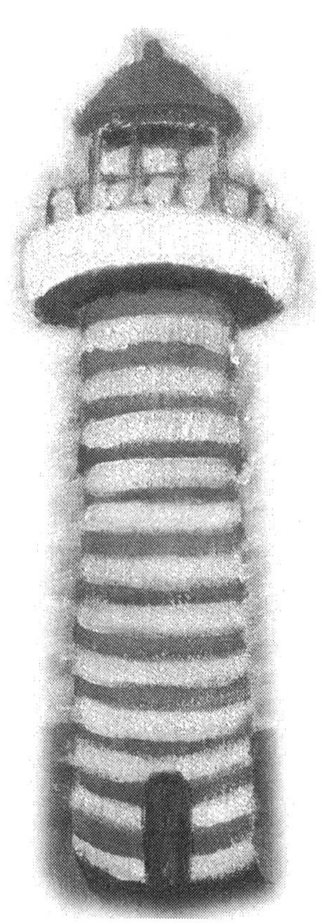

Cover Art by

Rod Boston

Carpe Diem, Mañana

Paul Lyons

Editor:

Dan Marcus

ISBN: 978-0-578-13330-0
Printed in the United States of America

Contents

Dedication

This book is dedicated to my dad, may he rest in peace.... He's alive, just always napping. Pop was there for my first comedy show and said, "Paul, I have never been so proud in my life." He continues to support me and inspire me. Pop was a mailman. His mailbag contained letters and bills, but also a Walter Brennan dummy which he would take out to entertain everyone. He delivered joy.

Thanks, Pop, for showing me the value of laughter and how to love life.

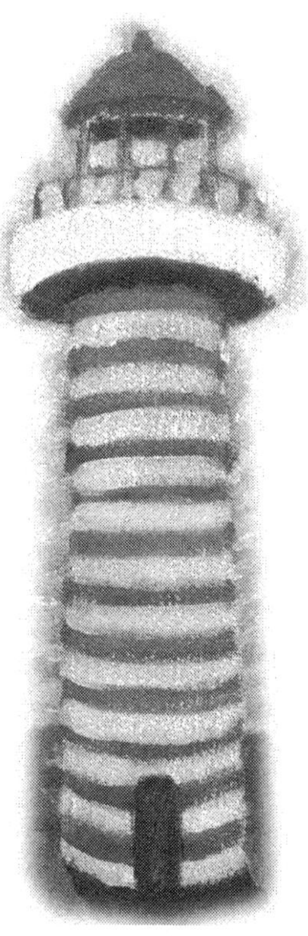

"Results! I have gotten a lot of results. I know several thousand things that won't work."

Thomas A. Edison

"Freedom is the only worthy goal in life. It is won by disregarding things that lie beyond our control. We cannot have a light heart if our minds are a woeful cauldron of fear and ambition. Authentic happiness is always independent of external circumstances. Vigilantly practice indifference to external circumstances. Your happiness can only be found within."

Epictetus (A.D. 55-135)

Sit Down, Enlighten Up

Recently, I began meditating. Actually, I sit and fall asleep. At first, meditation seemed ridiculous. There's so much to do, so little time. It's one of the lovely paradoxes of life: when I let everything go, I see I have everything I need. And there's something about doing nothing that cheers me up- like taking the day off. It's the same joy I feel when something on my to-do list gets canceled. Yes! I have more free time. Meditation brings me to that place of seeing I have all the time in the world. I don't need to do anything. And when I meditate, I don't sit on the floor cross-legged; I prefer a nice, comfy chair.

I set out looking for the perfect chair. I wandered into a tiny run-down thrift store, and there between the three-legged coffee table and the stack of *National Geographic* was the Green Chair. I sat down. I eased forward and the chair rocked. I leaned back and the chair reclined. "Damn," I thought, "flexibility turns me on."

"How much?" I asked.

"Ten dollars," the clerk said.

"Ten?"

The manager needed to get rid of it; it was blocking the aisle. I disguised my excitement and muttered about its girth. We settled on eight. How could anyone have passed it up? It's beautiful, it's adaptable, and according to its label it has a reputation for being Easy. And we have so much in common. How often women have looked at me as if I were blocking the aisle.

Sitting in my green bean, I've learned to be quiet, to listen. Outside, planes putter by. Wind chimes syncopate and rhyme. Why do birds suddenly appear? The breeze saunters in through the open window and caresses its way through my hair on a surprisingly warm day in March. I hear cars change gears to make their way up the hill. Never have I uttered "aah" so often, so openly, so shamelessly. I take it all in. At first from a 90-degree angle, then from 120 degrees, until finally I let it all come and go from 180 degrees: my head back, my feet up, and my nose nowhere near the grindstone.

Why are there are no love songs about the pleasures of a pleasant perch? No *Hey There, La-Z-Boy*? I'm willing to bet that behind every successful man is a lounger. My dad and I never had that talk. He never sat me down to tell me how great it was that we just sat down.

When I meditate in my chair I die to all the thoughts bossing me around. Carpe diem, mañana. No need to take life over, I can take life in. Meditation puts me firmly in the moment. How little I need to be happy. The green chair is just what I needed. Greenie gives me permission to slow down. All my life I've been striving to get somewhere. In my chair I know I'm already there. Aah.

They say if you want to feel good about yourself you need to set goals you can achieve. So my goals for this year are to

be in debt

and

not get laid.

All of a sudden I am a winner! I can't lose! Every time a woman walks away—success! My creditors call me up and say,

"Mr. Lyons, you are six months behind."

I say,

"That's right."

They ask why and I say,

"Because I am a man of my word."

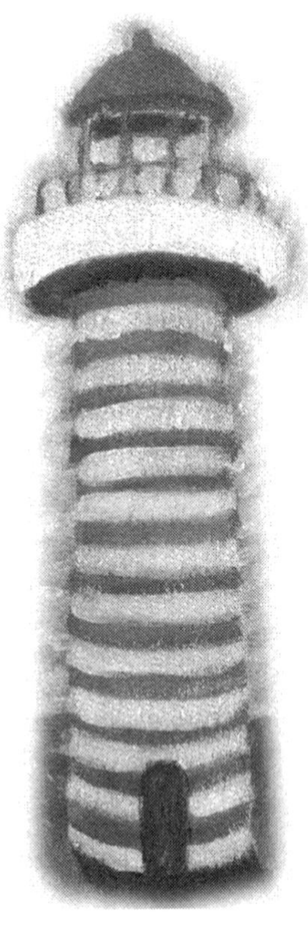

"Almost anybody can learn to think or believe or know, but not a single human being can be taught to be. Why?
Because whenever you think or you believe or you know, you are a lot of other people; but the moment you are being, you're nobody-but-yourself.
To be nobody-but-yourself—in a world which is doing its best, night and day, to make you everybody else—means to fight the hardest battle which any human being can fight; and never stop fighting.
Does this sound dismal? It isn't. It's the most wonderful life on earth. "

E.E. Cummings

How to Be a Paranoid Optimist

I have an active imagination with scenarios constantly swinging from horrific to heroic. I call it Paranoid Optimism. It's the *Murphy's Law* of spirituality: anything that can go wrong will go wrong, but fortunately it's all for the best. As a kid this thinking helped me fall asleep by assuming that the monster under my bed could beat the crap out of anyone in the closet.

I don't see the glass as half-empty; I see it as half-full- of the norovirus. I also imagine it tipping over and shattering. Luckily, one of the shards of glass slashes the foot of the thug about to mug me. As I bandage him up, I tell him it was no accident that we've met. He's been living in scarcity and should try on the notion of abundance. We become friends; he ends up selling me health insurance. Grateful, he gives me an affordable policy.

Ninety percent of what we worry about never comes to pass, which makes me worry. What's the 10 percent I should be worried about? I believe every pain near my heart is an oncoming heart attack. My left arm is constantly numb from testing it every three minutes. As soon as I read about an illness or medical condition, I develop the symptoms. I break out in a sweat and hives.

I've endured hepatitis, sickle cell anemia, and a yeast infection. I am a survivor . . . of my own delusions. I'm only able to picture the best after I've assumed the worst. When I get a headache I think: tumor! But then I imagine the silver lining. They've discovered good cholesterol, good fat. I could be the first person to get good cancer.

When I see a doctor, after the tests he'll call to say, "Paul, are you sitting down?"

"Yes, I am."

"Well, you'd better stand up. I've never had news like this before."

"I don't have cancer?"

"Oh, no, you have cancer; your body is riddled with cancer. But your cancer burns fat and builds muscle. In two weeks you'll be fit as a fiddle."

They will name my miraculous cancer after me. Doctors will break the news this way: "Sir, you're lucky. You have cancer."

"That's good news?"

"It's Paul Lyons cancer. It's an abnormal growth in consciousness. You can get out of bed every morning and move your body any way you like."

"But Doc, can't everyone do that?"

"Sure, but who does?"

"What about my heart palpitations?"

"Why, that's opportunity knocking! Wait till you meet the nurse who works the defibrillator."

Most of our assumptions are negative. And the truth is you never know. I recently had my identity stolen.

He improved my credit!

This guy is good. He calls my dad every week. He sends my girlfriend flowers. Thanks to him I am finally living up to

my full potential.

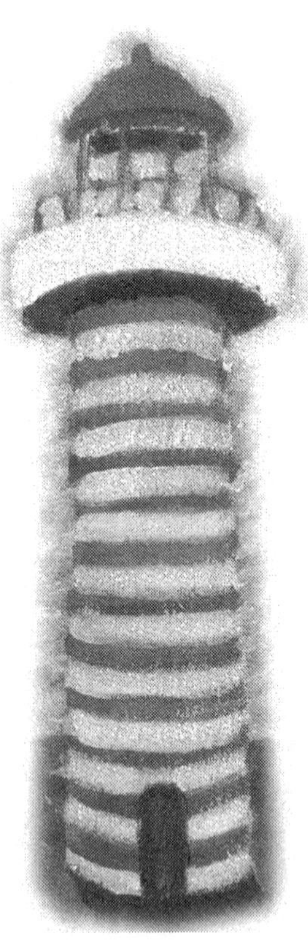

"Until one is committed there is hesitancy, the chance to draw back, always ineffectiveness. Concerning all acts of initiative (and creation) there is one elementary truth the ignorance of which kills countless ideas and splendid plans: that the moment one definitely commits oneself, then providence moves too. A whole stream of events issues from the decision, raising in one's favor all manner of unforeseen incidents, meetings and material assistance, which no man could have dreamt would have come his way."

W. H. Murray

Get Things Done

"License and registration, please." Caught speeding, I plead my innocence to the officer, emphasizing what a responsible driver I've always been. I open the glove compartment to get my registration and five tickets tumble out. He's a gung-ho cop, badge on his chest. No shirt, just a badge. He asks me if I know why he pulled me over. "Umm, quota?"

I often go too fast and I am rarely satisfied. And at the end of each day I'm miserable and spent. I focus on what went wrong, what I didn't accomplish, on the lack of check marks on my to-do list. I'm often trying to write a to-do list for the next day that will launch my life into the stratosphere. Carpe diem! When I wake up, I look at the list and think, "Who's going to do all this crap?" Well, by the end of the day, evidently not me. The only action I take on my list is to cross out Tuesday and write in Wednesday. Carpe diem, mañana. Looking back on my life, my biggest regret is that I didn't slow down and enjoy each day, each moment. Lately, my mantra each morning is to let nothing ruin my day. Doing more seems to mean enjoying less. I'd like to do less and enjoy it more. No matter what I do, or don't do, I will focus on what I *can* do.

Looking in my mirror yesterday I noticed excess flesh hanging over my belt. I said that's it! I went out and got bigger pants. I now have my to-do list set me up to win and to create momentum. I just write down everything I was going to do anyway:

Wake up. Done!

Hit snooze. Done!

Eat a bagel. Done!

Digest bagel. Done!

Take a nap. Done!

Wake up. (optional) Double Done!

Lose some hair. Done!

Enlarge my prostate. Done!

Grow ear hair. Done!

Wow, I'm a winner! Bring on the margaritas and the big pants.

Some curse the darkness.

I see an opportunity for **looting**.

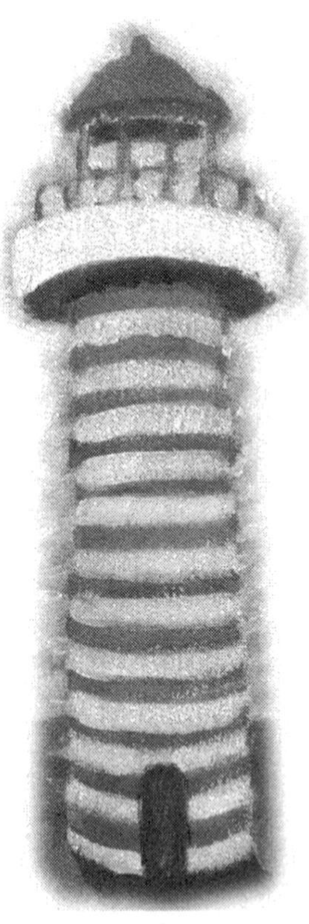

"Whatever you can do, or dream you can, begin it. Boldness has genius, power and magic in it."
Goethe

Learning to Fly with Elbow Room

I knew it would be a rough flight when I got a glimpse of the pilot. He'd missed a belt loop. Earlier, security had noticed something suspicious in my carry-on and sent it to be x-rayed again. Four guards converged and asked me what the black spot on my bag was. I could only guess. "A tumor?" It turned out to be toothpaste. They confiscated the 8-ounce tube. It's a shame we can't fight terrorism and cavities simultaneously. But as we all know, cleanliness is next to jihadliness.

While sitting in my exit row window seat the flight attendant asked, "Are you willing to operate the emergency door in the unlikely event of a water landing?" "More than willing," I said. "Doesn't even have to be a water landing. Be glad to do it anytime." Any idiot can volunteer for the exit row. A terrorist could sit by the emergency door, open it, and cause an unlikely city landing. Unless he gives himself away by packing *Aquafresh.* As I'm left to contemplate, a well-fortified man plumps down into the middle seat. The walk down the aisle has worn him out. What's he going to do in an emergency? Plug up a hole? As he sinks into his seat his arm invades our shared armrest, advancing into my territory. I feel like Poland in 1939. Where's Churchill? I close my eyes and think of England.

Maybe he'll fail the exit row interview. No such luck. He's able to nod both chins. Meanwhile, I can't get him to move his arm. I try nudging. Nothing. I'm thinking, "People like him are what's wrong with America!" Then I catch myself: "Paul, Don't condemn; look for the lesson. You need to speak up. Simply say, "Is it okay if we share the armrest?" But I don't speak up. I just hate the sweaty bastard.

I have a cup of coffee, which makes me hyper, and then I crash. I dream I'm playing basketball and the ball is coming toward me. My arms, not realizing it's a dream, fly up to catch it. The armrest Nazi jerks his body away from me, glaring at me as I try to explain, "The ball." He sneers and crosses his arms. I slide my elbow onto the armrest.

I learn a valuable lesson. Follow your dreams.

My friend Anita Wise found herself complaining that all of her joints creak and crack and pop.

Then she decided to look at what she can do.

Now Anita is doing great! She's making a little extra money as an exotic dancer for the blind.

She's not a whiner, she's a winner!

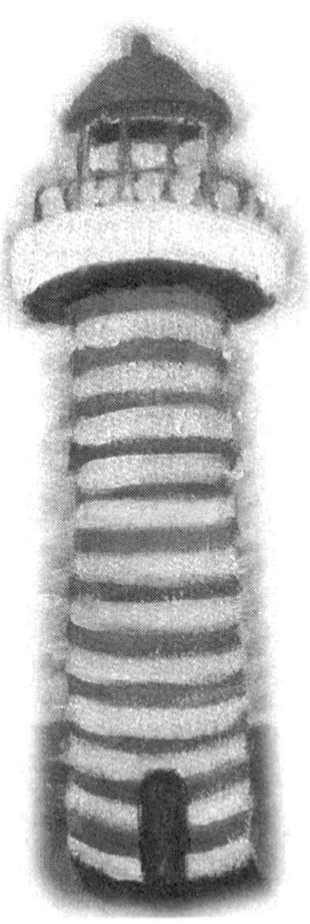

"That which doesn't kill you
makes you stranger."
Judith Greentree

How to Avoid Self-Improvement

Years ago I took EST (the Erhart Seminars Training, now Landmark Education). In one weekend I came to see how fearful we are of each other and how much I'd been living for other people's approval.

That first weekend was a share-fest. Everyone was opening up about the horrible things that happened to them. We learned that we were carrying those hurts around with us and that was closing us off from life. In my case, I had a chip on my shoulder because my dad used to call me lazy. Not exactly an act of brutality, but I was a sensitive kid (and I was lazy). Most of my life I'd blamed him for my lack of confidence, for my fear.

The course helped me to realize the positive side of my parents. They'd actively encouraged my desire to go into stand-up comedy (weekly newspaper clippings from my dad about the comedy business and Mom always reminding me that Bob Hope was also the fifth son of seven boys). In a fit of hysterical tears I called them up and poured out how much I appreciated all they had done for me. And for the first time, I said the words that were never spoken in our house: "I love you." My dad was taken aback and said, "Okay, okay." He would have been more comfortable if I was calling from jail. But like a drunk, I couldn't hold back; I loved the world and was overflowing with possibility. I was also fulfilling one of the main tenets of est: sharing. I wanted everyone to experience this new way of looking at life and felt sorry for all the people who didn't have the awareness that est provided.

I constantly tried to enroll my family. I was like a Jehovah's Witness, only worse. I was already inside the house; they couldn't pretend not to be home. I also shared est with all my friends. I invited Ray Romano to a meeting. He declined. Too bad, he could have made something of himself. I didn't see the irony in the idea that this organization promised to bring me more and more freedom as long as I kept taking more and more courses.

I thought that following their programs would allow me to live large. In many ways I was: I ran a marathon; I got a TV show produced. I was speaking honestly and sharing myself more than ever. What est didn't do was examine itself or encourage me to examine my relationship to it. The purpose of every organism and organization is survival and est put its own interest ahead of the participants. It found a way to keep us dependent.

As Helen Keller once said, "Security is mostly a superstition. It does not exist in nature nor do the children of man experience it on the whole. Life is either a daring adventure or nothing at all." Her words truly inspire me. Yesterday, for instance, I buttered my toast with my non-dominant hand. And I shared that with my proud parents.

Life is either a

struggle

or a

wiggle.

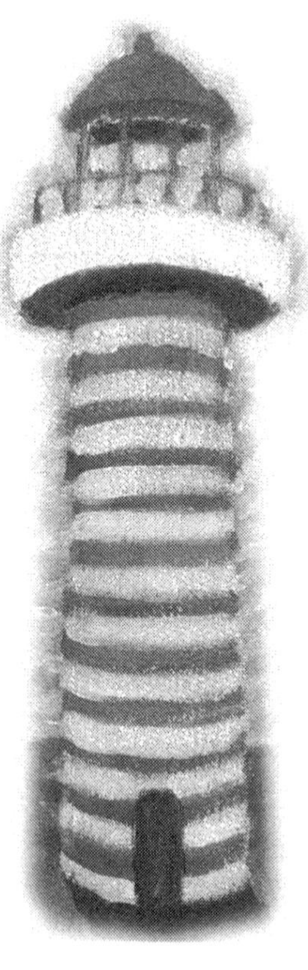

"We submit to authority because all of us have this inward demand to be safe, this urge to be secure. So long as we want to be secure-in our possessions, in our power, in our thoughts-we must have authority, we must be followers. This is very difficult for most of us because it means being insecure, standing completely alone, searching, groping, never being satisfied, never seeking success. But if we seriously experiment with it, then I think we shall find that there is no longer any question of creating or following authority because something else begins to operate- which is not a mere verbal statement but an actual fact. The man who is ceaselessly questioning, who has no authority, who does not follow any tradition, any book or teacher, becomes a light unto himself."

Jiddu Krisnamurti

Recovering from Purim

As a comedian I perform everywhere—last March at a Purim celebration for a few dozen Orthodox octogenarians. I went to shake the hand of the rabbi's wife. I got my first laugh, "We don't shake hands with men." So I offered her a fist pump. She laughed again. That was my last laugh of the night. Judging from the audience response, Purim is a celebration of silence.

Before the show started, I thought the rabbi looked nervous only to realize he was davening. Then he got onstage and read for about twenty minutes in Hebrew from a large scroll. He read the story of Esther and how she saved the Jews from destruction. Everyone seemed bored until the rabbi mentioned Haman. Then they went wild like in a scene from Awakenings, shouting and twirling their noisemakers. After his presentation the rabbi announced that the buffet was now open, and then, introduced me. As the old show business adage goes, never share the stage with animals, children, or gefilte fish.

Winging it I said, "How about a big hand for Esther!" Nothing. Maybe Esther was in the audience—most of these people may have known her personally. I mentioned I was single and a woman perked up. "Can you drive at night?" She got a laugh! Then they got quiet again. Very quiet. I banged on the microphone: "Is this thing on . . . or is it Shabbat?" Nothing. No one looked up from the buffet. I didn't know how to win them over. Winging it, I began chanting Haman! Haman! Haman! And I left on a festive, raucous note.

On my way out I let the rabbi know I was available for Yom Kippur.

I have a lousy HMO for my eye care; they have me go to an **optimist**. Here's the bright side: every visit he tells me,

"Everything's okay."

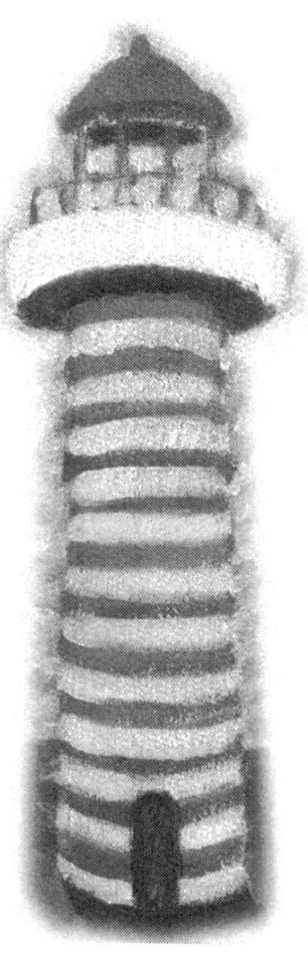

"Why should we be in such desperate haste to succeed, and in such desperate enterprises? If a man does not keep pace with his companions, perhaps it is because he hears a different drummer. Let him step to the music which he hears, however measured or far away."

Henry David Thoreau

Love Never Grows Old

"Paul. I like that name," the older woman resembling Sophia Loren said as she read my license at the DMV.

I told her I didn't care for it. "It's too plain."

She looked up, her lower lip thick and pouting, and said,

"Try living with Ruth."

"I'd like that," I said, "but maybe we should try dancing first."

"Oh, you're bad," she replied with a light, tinkling laugh. "I'm probably twice your age."

"And I'm probably twice your weight," I said. "Age is an arbitrary measurement."

She thought I was joking. I wasn't. I am a man who agrees with the line: "A thing of beauty is a joy forever. Its loveliness increases." Radiant, her ocean-green eyes beamed at me, only highlighted by the lines of time, which surrounded them. Her slender, loose-skinned neck begged for a soft caress and a gentle bite.

Older women are generally more eager to share their unbridled sensuality. Springtime may be sweet, but the flames of autumn more fiercely burn. Most men want to hold on to youth. Not me. I was thirty-three; I admired age. Each new year brings me more ease. At my 20th high school reunion, I not only spoke with Betsy Spendal without stuttering, I asked her to the prom. I was two husbands and six kids too late, but at least I made the effort. In my younger years, my view of life was myopic. My life was all about me. Now, I can see life all about me.

Age has been a rising hot air balloon, giving me a wider perspective. Ruth told me her age. Sixty-six. Wow, she's up there, I thought. I was as excited as a freshman who'd just landed a date with a senior, in this case, a senior citizen. If it's acceptable for an old man to date a much younger woman, why is it so absurd for a young man to date a much older woman? She fascinated me. How does she kiss? What's her passion, her history? What can I learn from her?

She sighed, "You know, I can't find men my age to dance with. They're all fuddy-duddies." Her frisky eyes took me in. "I used to be a dancer," she added wistfully.

"You're still a dancer. Ruth, let's go out sometime."

She leaned over, her ample breasts hovering just above my wanton fingertips. "You're not serious!"

"Yes, I am."

"I can't believe this. I've got slippers older than you."

"Then buy some new ones. Age is just . . ."

"An arbitrary measurement?"

"I like your spirit," I said. "Can I give you a call?"

She smiled and wrote down her number. Wow! On the phone that night our offbeat philosophies flowed together into an ocean of anticipation. A river ran through me.

"Ruth, I realize this is odd, our age difference and all, but I'm very attracted to you." I was certain she would squelch my ridiculous talk.

"I'm attracted to you, too," she giggled.

Goodness gracious! Great balls of fire! We set up a date. I made the mistake of telling a few friends. "Sixty-six years old? You'll break her hip." "Man, that's a real gray area." "Well, at least she can't get pregnant." "Make sure you whisper in her good ear." I told them I was looking at the bright side. I could take her to a movie and dinner for half-price. I'm an optimist. "Yes," a friend added, "your glass is half full, with her teeth in it."

I knocked on her door. We embraced, her breasts pressed against my chest, my bear-like arms locking us in the moment. "Oh boy," she purred. "Let's go."

The crowd was dancing at Big Al's Corral. We cut a rug, footloose and fancy-free, two misfits fit to be tied. Afterwards, we enjoyed a cozy Italian dinner and shared a bottle of wine. Then it happened: we smooched. Her kiss was full of passion as her tongue skated across my teeth. When we got back to her place, she made tea. Jazz music, her passion, swept through the room. We danced. She sang. My lips caressed her shoulders, her neck. We swooped to the floor. She bruises easily so we moved to the bedroom.

In the next few encounters I learned more about her. She was an insatiable lover, a nimble dancer, a jazz scat singer, a giving heart, a wounded daughter, a concerned mother, a lonely divorcée, a lost soul, a tender spirit, a fiery sunset.

While we were making out and groping one night she stopped, looked in my eyes, and said, "What do you want to do?" I was confused—we were already doing what I wanted to do. Did she want to stop and play Scrabble? Then it occurred to me: she wanted me to talk. Oh no! For years I never said a word in bed; I'd just make grunting sounds, like "uhh." Women weren't sure if I was having a good time or a cramp. But Ruth wanted to hear me verbalize what I wanted to do. I tried expressing what I liked about her: "I love your breasts. I love your big, bountiful breasts." It didn't sound sexy at all. I was using alliteration. I sounded like I was in a library. What would I say next? "Oh Ruth, I love your mammary glands." "Oh baby, who's your paternal unit?"

In the end, Ruth got me to open up. With her I learned to feel free and easy, where before with other women I'd generally felt anxious. She taught me so much. Our time together whetted my romantic appetite and gave me a glorious glimpse into the future, helping me to appreciate what getting older could mean. It left me yearning to touch another person's life, and to allow that life to touch mine.

I've always liked older woman, cougars. But now I'm fifty-three, and a woman much older than me can no longer be called a cougar.

She is more like a pterodactyl.

She'll show up in her scooter, take me home, and knit me a condom. Which is lucky for me, because

it takes thirty minutes for my pill to kick in.

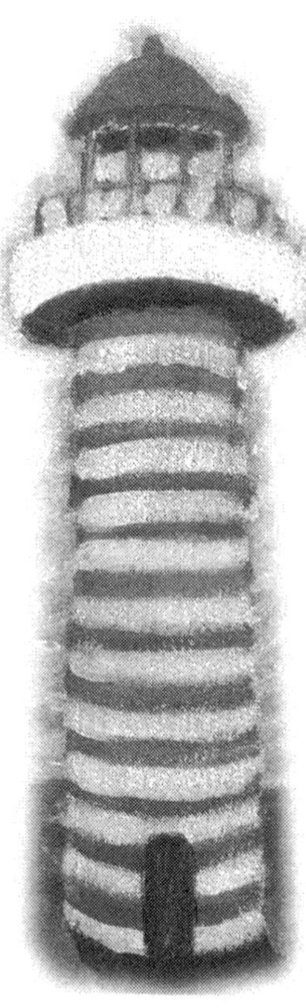

"May my mind come alive today
To the invisible geography
That invites me to new frontiers,
To break the dead shell of
yesterdays,
To risk being disturbed and
changed.

May I have the courage today
To live the life that I would love,
To postpone my dream no
longer
But do at last what I came here
for
And waste my heart on fear no
more."

John O'Donohue

Carpe Donut

There aren't many things in life that compare with the thrill of gazing into a bakery's display case: éclairs, critters, crème-filled, jelly-filled, full-figured, glazed, sprinkled, powdered, puffed, and plain. (Plain ones are surprisingly tasty due to lowered expectations.) One of the first privileges I indulged in when I became an adult and could support my longings was buying donuts. And not just one. Any kid can have one donut. But as an adult, the number of sweet treats you're permitted to have is endless. And you can eat them before dinner; you can eat them after dinner; you can eat them for dinner. You can even eat them and go swimming without having to wait thirty minutes.

I am a donut junkie whose habit on a bad binge only costs three bucks a day. With that kind of addiction, it's a long, delicious road before you hit bottom. And I have it under control. I realize that most addicts talk this way, but I've never missed a day of work because of my habit. Could I live the rest of my life without fried pastry? Yes, but why? Besides, there's nowhere to turn for help—every twelve-step program I've wandered into serves donuts. Some nights I park in front of Krispy Kreme with my headlights turned off. I try to convince myself that it's okay. I am worthy; I deserve it. The shop's neon sign is blinking at me: "Come in . . . enjoy . .

. you can take your pick. Someday, like when you're dead, you won't be able to do this."

"But I just had a Cinnabon yesterday."

"Who cares! Today is the first day of the rest of your fritters."

When I'm at the supermarket, after buying the obligatory fruits and vegetables, I'll add a box of glazed *Munchkins* to my cart. I can see the doughy treats through the see-through top. I can't help it, six *Munchkins* are eaten before I get to the check-out counter, four more before I've unpacked the grocery bags. Disgusted with my lack of control, I toss the remaining Munchkins in the trash. Three hours later, I dig through the garbage and retrieve them. I knew I would. That's why I threw them out in the box. I'm always one step ahead of me. My friend, Debbie said to spray the box with *Raid* before throwing it out. That taught me something. Raid doesn't taste too bad. A quitter never wins and a winner never quits eating donuts.

As a kid there was so little I could do. All I ever heard was

"no, you can't."

Now I say,

"Yes, I can!"

It's great to be an adult. I was home the other day playing with matches. Right before dinner I had a cookie. I'll go up to strangers and ask for candy:

"Hey pal, is that a Kit Kat? Can I have a piece? Sure, I'll go for a ride with you."

Yes, I can. Because a winner takes chances!

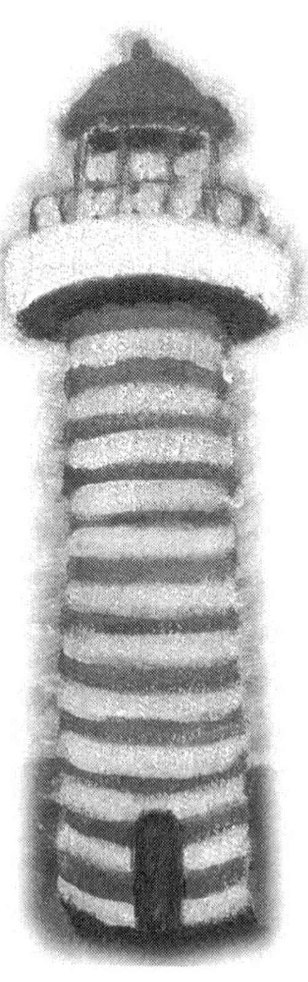

"Our life is frittered away by detail. . . I say, let your affairs be as two or three, and not a hundred or a thousand; keep your accounts on your thumbnail. . . . Simplify, simplify. Instead of a hundred dishes, five; and reduce other things in proportion."

Henry David Thoreau

The Move-the-Scale Diet

Every year I gain about five pounds. Last year I weighed 193. I thought, "This is disgusting." I resolved to start a diet after Christmas, but failed to select a year. When I got on the scale yesterday, it read 198. Now I'd like to lose five pounds so I can get back to being disgusting. I began feeling better when I realized at the rate I'm going I weigh five pounds less than I will next year!

Weight control is no piece of cake, though in my case it often is several pieces. My bank has a jar of free "fun-size" candy. Candy companies sure know how to lure us back. Fun-size. Is anyone anti-fun? How bad can a mini-box of Junior Mints be? When it's free and small, it never seems like calories. I found myself going to the bank three times a day.

"Hello, Mr. Lyons, are you making a withdrawal?"

"Yes, a mini-*Snickers*, please."

Lately, I've discovered a way to lose weight. My friend, Mim said, "Paul, I weigh myself twice every morning. The first time is always disappointing, but then I move the scale around the bathroom and find a spot where I weigh a pound less." And I found that when I put the scale on a thick throw rug, voilà, I'm three pounds lighter. And if I want to get back to my old high school weight, I lean against the wall. Wow, I just earned a donut! I'll dig through the trash.

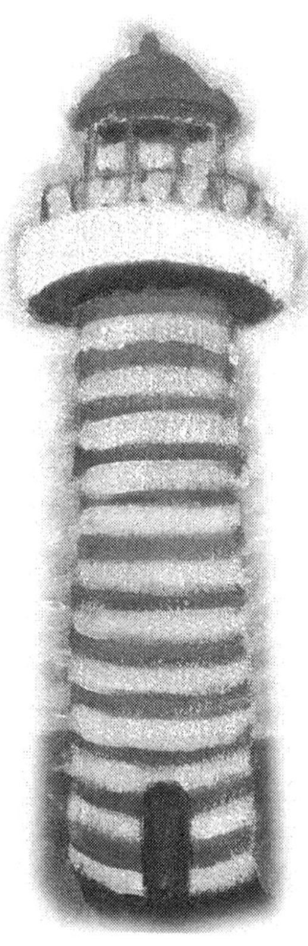

"The fool who persists in his folly becomes wise."
William Blake

How to Enjoy a Cookie

"Cookies and pretzels? Cookies and pretzels?" I hear the flight attendant's voice as she makes her way down the aisle. I love Delta's biscotti cookies. Crisp and flat, with a burst of cinnamon. What a great flight! I have the whole row to myself. I can stretch out and relax. I'm doing better than first class, packed because so many people got upgraded. Great, more room for me and my cookies.

When she reaches my row, the flight attendant asks, "What would you like to drink?"

"Tea, please," I answer, very happy about my healthy choice. And it goes s well with the cookies.

"I'll have to come back," she says. And off she goes.

I don't get offered a cookie? I don't get a second drink option? I'm thirsty. I'm hungry. Why did she offer cookies to everyone else and not me?

"Excuse me," I say. She doesn't respond. My hand flails. "Excuse me," I say more loudly. Nothing. I'm furious now. What happened? In one second I've gone from tickled pink to hissy fit. She's still only two rows away. If I don't get her now, she'll go up the whole rest of the cabin before she gets back to me. She must hear me, see my arm.

"Hello!" I'm shouting now.

"Just a minute," she snaps. "I'm with someone." Yes, she is, and she's offering him my cookies. "Hello, would you like Paul's cookies?"

I'm a happy-go-lucky guy until my expectations go unmet, which is constantly. As Sartre said, "Hell is other people." At least I think that's what he said. We were in a crowded Parisian café and his English was horrible. But here I am, trapped on this plane and I want to cry out, "Why didn't you ask me if I wanted cookies, or perhaps something else to drink?" Instead I sit and stew. Poor me. All we are is our latest thought. I notice how quickly I went to feeling slighted. Lucky Paul became Poor Paul. Why did she ignore me? I answer myself very wisely, "Paul, it may have nothing to do with you. She simply forgot to ask. She is busy feeding the whole plane." I start to calm down. I'm ready to go back to enjoying the flight. Then I hear her offer someone else my cookies.

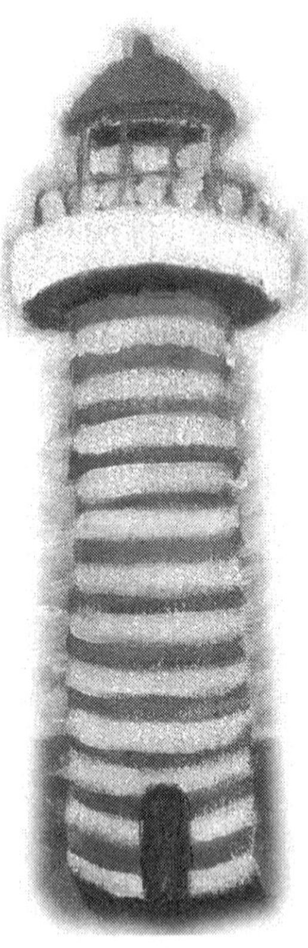

"No amount of self-improvement can make up for a lack of self-acceptance."
Robert Holden

The Cat in the Attic

It's 2:00 a.m. and something is scampering around in my attic. I think I know what it is. The other day I put birdseed in my window box, which attracted a beautiful cardinal, a glori- ous hummingbird, and a fat rat. When I spotted him, the fat rat bastard leaped onto the side of the building and clawed his way vertically to the roof like a comic book arch-villain.

I have a ten-by-ten square foot studio apartment. I keep it sparse so every Tuesday I can play racquetball. In my attic I store all the stuff I should be throwing out. I figure as long as I still have my stuff I didn't waste my money buying it. The attic holds fifteen years of bad decisions including a Snuggie, parachute pants, and a flowbee.

I enlarged a hole in the ceiling above my kitchen sink. To get to the attic I stand on my kitchen counter and lift myself up into the crawl space. Inevitably my shirt gets caught on an exposed rusty nail. The torn shirts get left up there like planted flags of a hard-won battle. People see the scar on my arm and ask, "Damn, what happened? Gunshot wound?" Sort of. I impaled myself on a *Magic Bullet.*

Everything in my attic is useless, a detention center for all things broken and reeking, lots of wood crates and books. A fire hazard? No worries there. Thanks to a leaky roof everything is soggy. And what could be more fitting than a damp edition of *Moby Dick*? My landlord doesn't see the porous roof as a problem either. He calls it ventilation.

It's now 2:30 a.m. and I've got to do something about that noisy, fat rat bastard. Aha! My cat, Leviticus, can scare him away. I'm a genius. I gingerly lift her up through the hole in the ceiling. Unfortunately, the only one scared is Leviticus. She walks a few feet into the attic then back to the opening, crying to get down. I try to grab her and she goes ballistic, scratching my arm and fleeing into the attic's interior. I've lost her trust. Leviticus is meowing now, loudly enough for the neighbors to hear. I place a bar stool on top of the kitchen counter so that it's a very short, easy jump down, but she begs to differ and continues meowing. I go back to bed assuming she'll eventually give in and jump. But a half an hour later she's meowing louder in a high-pitched whine that must be carrying for miles. I shriek at her, "Leviticus! Get Down! Leviticus! Get down! Leviticus! Get down!" I sound like a Holy Bay City Roller. I'm an idiot. What was I thinking?

I google "How to get a cat down from a high place." The first listing to appear is "How to get your cat high." I eventually find a site with a useful suggestion. I lift myself into the attic and Leviticus soon mellows and comes to get petted. I grab an old mildewed wicker hamper (thank God I saved it). She crawls into it and I close the lid. I look around at the boxes of cassette tapes, Mardi Gras beads, and books on MS-DOS. It's chilly. I put on a frayed *Members Only* jacket. It's now 4 a.m. I'm huddled in a crawl space on a George Foreman grill next to a hamper containing my cat. And wonder why I'm still single.

I lower the hamper onto the counter, get myself down, lower the cat onto the safety of the floor, open the lid, and she bounces out. I go back to bed. The rat's still scampering around. What can I do? I decide to call him Jared. Good night Leviticus. Good night Jared. Tomorrow's Tuesday. After I shove the beanbag chair into the attic: racquetball!

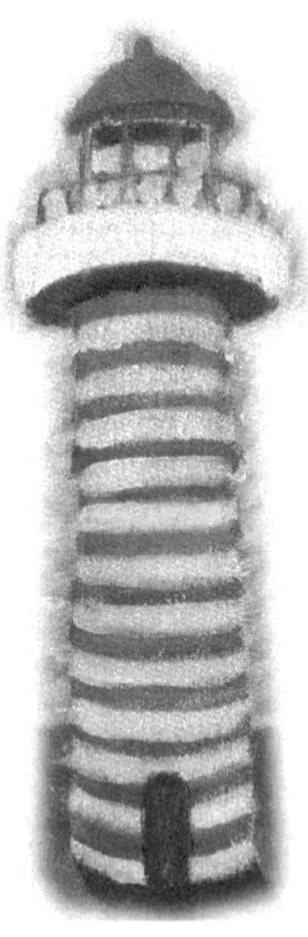

"If at first you don't succeed, change your definition of success."
Richard Stockton

Look at What You *Can* Do

Success is all about how we respond to challenges. Unfortunately, we don't usually learn those things in school. Instead, we learn so-called problem-solving skills like algebra. Why not teach that there are no problems, only opportunities? Every math teacher insists that we'll need algebra someday. When? I've never run into x in my life. But since they taught it to me, I use it.

When I pull into a gas station, I go up to the attendant and say: "I left Chicago this morning at 6 a.m., driving 55 miles per hour. My brother Theodore left in a motorboat, doing 12 knots per hour. How many quarts of oil will we need? And show all your work."

I think school should teach how our minds operate. What we focus on grows and we seem to constantly be looking at what's wrong, when we could be looking at what's working. We could be looking at what we *can* do.

What a wonder our lives are! When we're upset we'll stand there flailing our arms for fifteen minutes railing about the evils of the world without realizing, "Wow, I can flail my arms! I am the boss of my body." I've come to appreciate all my body can do, because sometimes there are things it can't do. The other day my back hurt so much, I dropped a dollar and couldn't pick it up. I had to pay a kid five dollars to retrieve my buck.

Now whenever I remember I relish all the parts of my body that I can move. I'm always ready to bust a groove. But when I go to dance clubs, everyone is so young. I walk in and the music stops. "Oh no, we're getting audited." "Hell no," I say. "Put another dime in the jukebox, baby. I love the nightlife. I love to boogie."

I'm still hip. I was out on the dance floor, dancing by myself and having a blast. A young woman joined me so I immediately started doing my old-school moves, like The Sprinkler. Well, I must have gotten tangled up in the hose. I fell over. When I turned around she was gone. Maybe she was a paramedic checking up on me. Then I looked down and there she was, still dancing, bent over and touching the ground with her hands. She was twerking! I asked, "Can you get my dollar?" She just shook her booty and backed into me. She was all in my business. It's a small business, but it's my business. And as she was grinding away I'm thinking, "Do I have to pay for this? Again?

Then her boyfriend came up to me and said, "Hey, pal, you got a problem?" I said, "Yeah, if a train leaves Chicago at 6 a.m. . . ."

There are no problems, only opportunities to annoy people.

You can't have low self esteem if you have a dog. I used to feel guilty about taking naps.

Not anymore.

Now every time I lie down my dog is like,

"Oh wow, that is such a great idea! How do you think of these things? Let me snuggle up next to genius!"

I'm not being lazy; I'm spending quality time with Charlie.

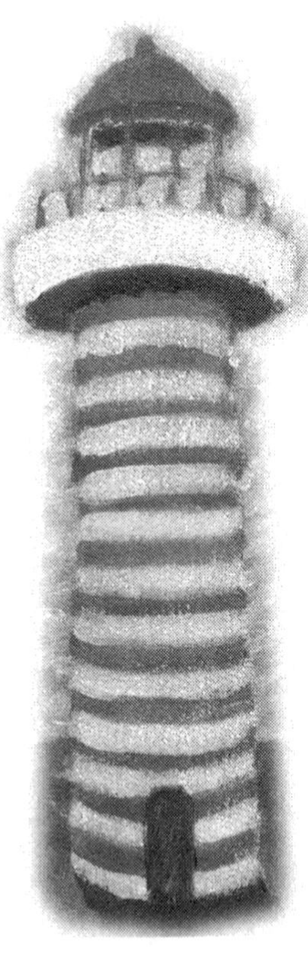

"Life, at it's best, is a flowing, changing process in which nothing is fixed. To experience this is both fascinating and a little frightening. I find that I am at my best when I can let the flow of my experience carry me, in a direction that appears to be forward, toward goals of which I am dimly aware. When I am thus able to be in process, it is clear that there can be no closed system of beliefs, no unchanging set of principles which I hold. Life is guided by a changing understanding of and interpretation of my experience. It is always in process of becoming."

Carl Rogers

How to Make Love Like a Professional Comedian

Sex is overrated. That's not just my opinion. Every woman I've slept with agrees. I tried to improve my sexual performance for many years, but being with a partner tended to cause more anxiety than pleasure, so I always looked for safe relationships in which to practice. This doesn't exactly make women want to jump in bed with you. Not for free anyway. (I would never pay for sex. And I think anyone who does just makes more money than I do.)

Over time I've learned a good lesson: the more I try to improve, the worse I get. If my focus is always on what's wrong, no matter what I improve I'll keep seeing the flaws. In my twenties, thinking I wasn't enough, I overcompensated sexually. I'd heard it's the motion of the ocean, so I would hop on top of her and go at it about a hundred miles an hour. I wasn't making love, I was making a tsunami. Afterwards we'd lie there smoking, from the rug burns. Now I know it's not good sex if your partner has to tap out.

These days I have a better understanding of women. They have a different tempo. It takes them a tad longer to be turned on. If I want to have some action on Friday I start on Tuesday. She's like a turkey. I have to baste her, pre-heat the oven, get a few side dishes going. I can't just show up and stuff it.

I've come to understand that the most important thing to focus on is not the performance, but our connection. Let her know how she turns me on. And at the end even if she fakes it, I can still gaze into her eyes and say, "That was a beautiful faux finish."

Some folks do death defying feats to feel fully alive. Not me. I nap. I wake up and think,

"Wow, I was gone like twenty minutes, got up, saw the light . . . then went over and turned it off. I'm alive and I'm not going to take it for granted. I'm going to live my dream, like the one I just had.

I was eating a burrito in my underwear with Nicki Minaj."

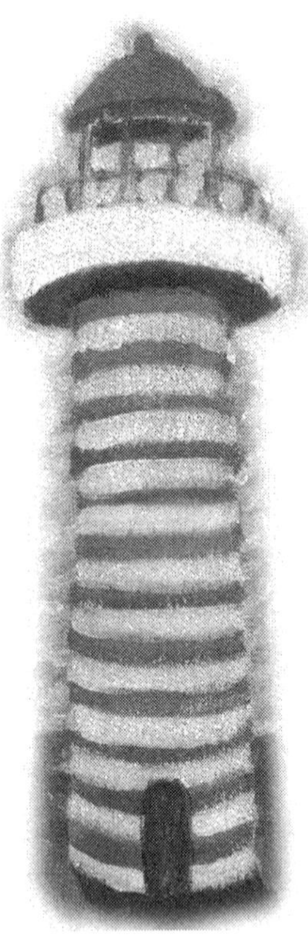

"There are only two ways to live your life. One is as though nothing is a miracle. The other is as though everything is a miracle."

Albert Einstein

My Ship Came In (and Sunk)

A thousand people are in their seats. This is the first day of their cruise to Mexico, a vacation they've saved all year for. And they've traveled all day to get here. It's 11:00 p.m. and I'm the comedian performing in their welcome-aboard show. Before introducing me, the cruise director lulls them into a catatonic stupor, then has them all stand up so they can get used to giving standing ovations. "You'll be seeing some exceptional shows," he announces, "and should show your appreciation with a standing ovation." No pressure for me!

Once I'm onstage people do start standing up; unfortunately they are on their way out. Did someone yell "Fire"? Normally, this situation would bring on severe distress. But today I decide to enjoy myself despite the audience reaction. I will love the audience, however unrequited. I focus on playing with my material and assume that those who've remained in their seats are laughing on the inside.

When I'm done I go over to the cruise director and remark, "Wow, that was the quietest crowd I ever had." He just mumbles, "Yeah, they uh, hmm, they uh, hmm . . ." I want to share my breakthrough: "Hey, I still had fun. I didn't sweat, didn't get all dry-mouthed. It didn't affect my self-esteem. I'm still a winner!" But he's already left the room.

Later, my glee melts into panic. Would any cruise ship ever book me and my quiet act again? Over the past two years I've expanded my career, paid off my debts, and made enough money for a down payment on a house. Soon I'll be able to shop at Whole Foods. I want the money to keep coming in. I was desperate to continue my financial success, believing that cruise ships were the only way I could make a decent living. But actually there are many places I can perform: clubs, casinos, maximum-security prisons, Purim celebrations. When I first got on the ships, I was hungry and continuously developing my craft. Now I had an act that I thought worked. But it no longer had passion. Another lesson learned. Failure is not a bad option. It showed me what I needed to fix. Continuing to build an act I love will direct me to the right audience and bring in the money. I don't have to depend on any one thing. As Steve Jobs said, "Stay foolish. Stay hungry." I have options. And there are plenty of ships I haven't bombed on. Yet.

The next night I felt my groove. I tried some new material that I really liked and it worked. It was a family show and an eight-year-old girl said she liked *SpongeBob SquarePants.* I said I don't like *SpongeBob. He*'s too self-absorbed. She said, "Well, you're self-absorbed too. You keep saying, I am a winner." I laughed and said, "You're right I am self-absorbed. I haven't stopped talking since I hit the stage." The young girl's mother said her daughter tends to talk a lot in school. And I responded, "That's what is so hard about school. When she was a baby and she started to walk everyone was so excited. 'Wow! Yes, you go girl!' Then she started to talk and everyone was delighted. 'Wow, she said Mommy. She said Daddy. She's talking. She's talking!' Then she gets to school and all she hears is, 'Sit down, and shut up.'"

And I got applause. Because I am a winner!

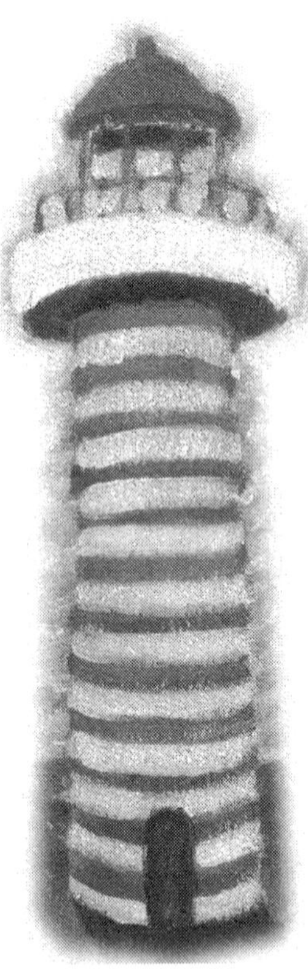

"Things themselves don't hurt or hinder us. Nor do other people. It is our reactions and attitudes that give us trouble. Therefore even death is no big deal. It is our notion of death, our idea that it is terrible, that terrifies us. There are many ways to think about death. Scrutinize your notions about death— and everything else. Are they doing you any good? Don't dread death or pain. Dread the fear of death or pain. We cannot choose our external circumstances, but we can always choose how we respond to them."

Epictetus (A.D. 55-135)

My Pop, a Mac Daddy

All of Pop's excess weight goes to his belly, but he brags that he still wears a size 32 waist. That's because he doesn't get his pants up past his fibula. He's wearing 32 x16 pants: capris. Pop shops at Chico's. He's always dressed with his pants low and his boxers hanging out. Pop was ahead of his time, a real trendsetter. He was the first gangbanger. Next year look for everyone to be wearing black socks with flip-flops. My dad will be leading the pack with his rap, "Put your hands in the air like you're on Medicare / Pants on the ground, a glass for my teeth / celebrated Easter with my marshmallow peeps."

Pop always gave the same advice: "Plan ahead." So I listened to him; I moved into a nursing home. It's working out, lots of single babes. They love it when I whisper in their good ear, "I can drive at night."

When I was sixteen, my dad thought it was time for us to have that talk. So he sat me down with my two kids: "Paul, be safe." That was it. I listened to him. Next time I was in the car with my girlfriend; we hopped into the backseat and I buckled up. "Safety first, Sheila."

Dad hates to waste money. The other day he said to me, "Paul, why should I spend $2,500 on a hearing aid? It costs me nothing to say, 'Huh?'" Recently, I wanted to mail Dad a birthday card. I went to the post office to get stamps. Thirty people in line. Damn, I could be waiting all day! I said to myself, "Paul, calm down. You can handle this. You are a winner!" And it came to me. I mailed my letter without a stamp. I just put my address in the center and my dad's address in the upper left-hand corner.

My dad is eighty-five and a widower. Barbara, the woman he's dating, wanted to meet his friends. So he said,

"Okay, we'll go see Chico and Pete at St. Dennis Cemetery, then go over to Calgary Cemetery to see Jesse and Kincade."

Death used to scare the hell out of him. He focused on all his friends dying, fearing his own death. He started living by accepting death, being happy to be alive, enjoying his friends who are still around, and learning to appreciate his eighty-eight year old buddy who's dating two women (if one croaks, he won't have to start from scratch).

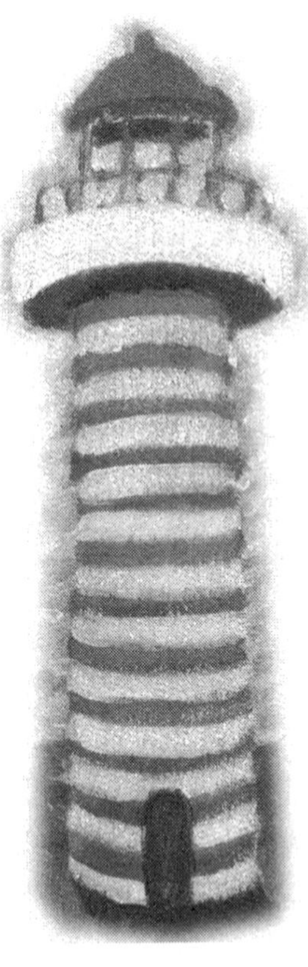

"It is something to be able to paint a particular picture, or to carve a statue, and so to make a few objects beautiful; but it is far more glorious to carve and paint the very atmosphere and medium through which we look... To affect the quality of the day, that is the highest of arts."

Henry David Thoreau

If At First You Don't Succeed

I'll do anything: dance at bus stops, run naked through cafeterias, approach two strangers and say, "You're an adorable couple. Should you ever break up, I would date either one of you." People ask, "You drunk?" No! I don't need booze. I don't want to depend on anything for courage. My life's mission: to see through fear's crippling illusions, to act in the face of fear, and to live with freedom. So imagine my surprise at finding myself in an alley at 10:35 a.m. on a Tuesday morning guzzling gin.

I'd left the doctor's office because I was about to flunk the drug test I needed to pass for my job working on cruise ships. No drugs in my system. I simply can't urinate under pressure. Under federal law the doctor must be in the bathroom to observe. He watched me for five minutes. I couldn't go. We tried three times over fifty minutes. Could not go. Jokingly, I asked if he could fill the cup for me. "Ah, you can do it!" More embarrassing than not being able to pee in front of a doctor is having him cheer you on. I haven't been cheered on to go to the bathroom since I was two. And I haven't been able to pee in public since I was eleven.

At a Phillies' game with hordes of men and boys standing in lines, I stepped up to the urinal trough and waited. And waited. Other lines kept moving; everyone behind me stood waiting. The crowd outside was booing, probably at me. After what seemed like an entire inning, I zipped up and walked away. Ever since that day I've used the bathroom stall. To hide my phobia I sit down. However, I have been able to use urinals on occasion after drinking.

Meanwhile, I've exhausted the doctor's excellent bedside manner and bathroom banter. "No rush," he said. "You'll pee eventually." That was over an hour ago. Each time it's the same scenario: standing in the hallway till I feel the urge, notifying the doctor, then bounding into the bathroom while he watches me do nothing. I tried running the faucet, thinking of waterfalls. I should have put one hand in a bowl of warm water and fallen asleep wearing a catheter.

Before long, the entire office knew about my predicament because I was standing in the hallway getting in their way. A beautiful nurse kept passing me. Finally, she asked, "Can you sit in the waiting room till you're ready?" Then it hit me: time for booze! If I wanted to pass my drug test I needed to get drunk. I walked outside to a market, bought a small bottle of gin, and crept down an alley swigging it down, ready to sing some blues. I saw a woman smoking outside a courthouse and said, "They gave you a break, huh?"

"Nope, I took it. Dealing with dumb ass criminals!"

"Yeah, prisons would be nicer with a better class of people." She smiled. I was impressed with my wit. And I felt great.

It's a wonderful world. A change of scenery always helps. And so does a good buzz.

Back in the waiting room I asked for the doctor, went in, tried not to burp, and filled up the cup. I did it! I don't know which one of us was more relieved. We practically high-fived. But I thought it better to wash my hands first.

I didn't give up. We all need a little help once in a while. Standards are often disappointments waiting to happen. I let go of my pride over never depending on alcohol. My notions of who I am don't have to be rigid. I shifted my standard and won- eventually. That's living with freedom. If at first you don't succeed, try, try a gin.

"The way to do is to be."
Lao Tzu (604-532 B.C.)

iLove My iLife

I'm the proud owner of a new MacBook Pro and iPhone. I see people with flip-phones and think, "There but for the grace of God go I. Come on, get with it. Turn on, drop out, and iTune in!" I'm a Mac Daddy. If only the world were run by Apple. Wait a minute, it is. After buying my previous Mac computer four years ago, I went in twice with a minor glitch and both times they said, "Rather then wait for us to fix it, just take a new computer." Really? What store does that? Impressed, I gave my Mac to a friend and eagerly purchased the latest MacBook Pro. A few months later I had to bring it in because I spilled a little soda on the keyboard, and fried everything. I wasn't going to tell them that. Using a hair dryer I was able to get the power back on, but the cursor kept going haywire, moving around like a mosquito and clicking on arbitrary websites. (That explains the bookmarks for sites featuring scantily-clad midgets.)

At the store's Genius Bar I was met by a kid of around twenty. Most be a prodigy! He took my computer apart and discovered the corrosion. "Something spilled on it," he stated calmly. Talk about jumping to conclusions. He added that it would cost $855 to get a new board.

I was taken aback. "Nothing spilled on it. I live in Santa Monica. There's a lot of morning dew. Perhaps some compensation seeped in. It's compensation!"

"That's 'condensation,' not 'compensation'," he said.

"That's condescension," I muttered.

"Sorry, sir, but water damage is not covered."

Did he have to call me "sir"? I was furious. I have to pay $855 because the computer can't handle dew? (Okay, it was *Mountain Dew.*) I demanded a second opinion and another young genius came over.

"That's corrosion damage caused by a spill."

I walked home, reeling from the shabby treatment. Then it occurred to me that I was lying. I spilled soda on it. I'd recently spent lots of money, overextended myself. My notion of living in abundance had left me broke. Now I was coming from scarcity. I remembered the first line in *The Road Less Traveled*: "Life is difficult." Wow, yes. Once I accept that every day brings problems, all I have to do is be willing to respond to them. Life is a mess, but the frame we put it in can make it manageable. I will be dead some day, will it matter that I paid $855 for a new board? Everything tends to work out (except the fact I'll be dead some day).

Then and there, I resolved to always tell the truth, keep beverages away from the keyboard, and move to a drier climate.

I'm surprised by the way people respond to the greeting,

"How's it going?"

Some say,

"Same old, same old."

Others say,

"Can't complain."

Why don't we appreciate life more? We don't talk that way at funerals:

"Too bad Jack can't be here for the same old same old. But on a happier note, at least he can't complain."

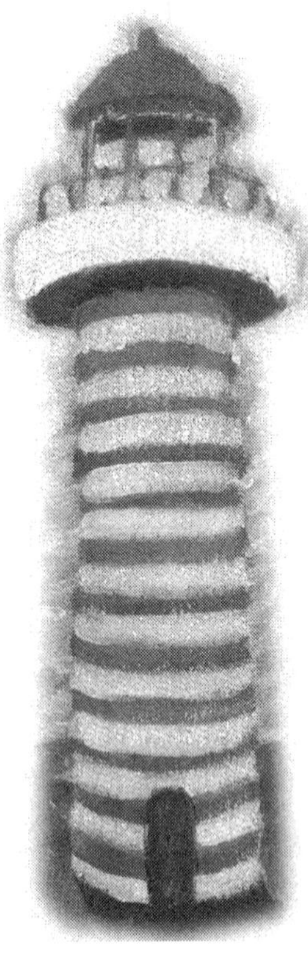

"If one advances confidently in the direction of his dreams, and endeavors to live the life which he has imagined, he will meet with a success unexpected in common hours."

Henry David Thoreau

The Healing Power of Nature

The book that has inspired me the most to follow my own path is *Walden.* And reading the book on my Nook is one thing; being at Walden is quite another. I've heard Thoreau's beckoning call. Said he, "A man is rich in proportion to the number of things he can afford to let alone." Indeed. I long for a life in the woods. Or at least a day. I was going to pitch a tent but I snagged an epic deal from *Groupon* at the *Red Roof Inn.*

Parking at Walden's welcome center, I splurge on a five-dollar "Save the Trees" bumper sticker and pick up a twenty-five page info packet. One pamphlet mentions a tram that will glide around the pond while another describes the Henry David Thoreau Unassisted Living Facility. I grab my backpack and a liter of *Smartwater*, then go a-gaping out into the wild. Alas! What a sheer delight. I love nature. My ring tone is whale song. O, the great outdoors! It's so pleasing to hear the sounds of these hallowed woods in the silences between the songs on my Pandora. This is just what the doctor ordered- solitude. To get off the grid! I needed this and so did all the people in front of me. Nature is so healing. I catch it on the *National Geographic Channel* as often as I can. I see a squirrel. Big deal, they're as common as *Dells.* It would be wicked to see a woodchuck or a muskrat. I must take a picture of these vines wrapped around the gnarly barks on these silver trunks. Or is it poison oak? Let's google it. I feel the breeze turning my cheeks red. Ah, the indescribable innocence and beneficence of nature. This trail is filled with scarlet maples and ancient spruces; it will look awesome after *Photoshop*. A maple leaf, electric maroon, falls and floats just like in 3-D.

Ah, dusk! The sun curtsies as its orange skirt rises above the horizon and eventide's purple curtain descends, casting its reflection onto Walden Pond's rippling stage. Bravo eve- ning! Bravo pond! Above me, dozens of hawks take flight with flapping applause. Behold the full moon, that drama queen, as she steals the nighttime show and reminds me that I am part of it all. I am alive. Talk of heaven! This pinecone will look sweet in my cubicle. Time to tweet: "Such feigned joy in taking life over, such pure joy is taking life in. I can see signs of God all around me." Yes. Okay. Let's see what Miley Cyrus is really pregnant.

Lo, the solace of the primeval forest. I am at one with everything. I am a PC and a Mac. Sauntering up a hill, I relish the explosion of wildflowers which twilight dusts in sepia. I bet someone is watching me now on *Google Earth*. I'll moon them. Ha! An owl serenades me: "to-whit, to-who, to-who." I rejoice as I scold him: "To whom! To whom!" Aah, such fun to tease the critters. Something rustles in the woods. I scurry back on the path. Terra firma! My heart beats, and I can now say it beats to its own drummer. It's been twenty-two glorious minutes. No phone calls. No texts. No emails. Wait, let me check. What am I doing?

Look at all the stars. It's amazing—it looks exactly like a planetarium. Except very chilly. Let's get the weather. Damn, it's dipped down to forty degrees. It's minus ten in Bangkok. Glad I'm not there. I'm all out of power bars. I need to get home. See what I missed.

I learned this, at least, from my sojourn: that if one walks confidently in the direction of one's dreams, skinny jeans tend to chafe the inner thighs. But, it's so worth it!

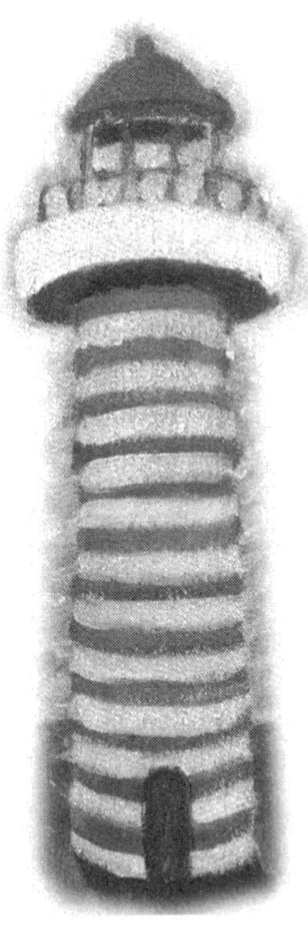

"I want a life that sizzles and pops and makes me laugh out loud. And I don't want to get to the end, or to tomorrow even, and realize that my life is a collection of meetings and pop cans and errands and receipts and dirty dishes. I want to eat cold tangerines and sing out loud in the car with the windows open and wear pink shoes and stay up all night laughing and paint my walls the exact color of the sky right now. I want to sleep hard on clean white sheets and throw parties and eat ripe tomatoes and read books so good they make me jump up and down, and I want my everyday to make God belly laugh, glad that he gave life to someone who loves the gift."

Shauna Niequist

The Healing Power of Google

I woke up sore and could barely walk because of an aching in my groin. I googled my symptoms. Then I rushed to the emergency room. The doctor walked in and I immediately explained my predicament.

"Doc, I have chlamydia."

"What makes you think you have that?" he asked.

"I googled 'swollen testicle' and that was the second and third thing to come up."

"What was the first?" he inquired.

"Miley Cyrus."

"That can't be good."

He examined me and concluded I had epididymitis, a relatively common infection. I used to take a doctor at his word, but not now, not with the Internet. These days it's amazing how much knowledge we have at our fingertips. In the '70s the only resource my family had was the Encyclopedia Britannica. Our edition was published in 1964. I did a school report in 1973 predicting that man would someday land on the moon. But today thanks to the Internet I'm much more informed. I didn't trust the doctor's flimsy conclusion and asked him to run a test for chlamydia.

"When did you have sex last?"

"Three months ago."

"I doubt you have it. If you did, you would have known sooner." He left the room to run some tests. I took the opportunity to get a second opinion from std.com on my iPhone. When he came back I shared my concern.

"Doc, 60 percent of men have chlamydia and don't even know it."

He corrected me: "Sixty percent of men don't have chlamydia. One percent of the male population has chlamydia and 60 percent of them don't know it. That's because most of them had sex in the past week."

Clearly the doctor was throwing me a zinger. I wanted to tell him that the reason I hadn't had sex in three months was because I am very particular. I will not have sex with a woman until she says yes. But still concerned, I told the doctor that chlamydia could lead to blindness.

"You wouldn't go blind."

"How about the May 2003 case reported in WebMD? The patient incurred acute ocular dryness and he went blind."

"The blindness could have stemmed from many factors. You have epididymitis. Take ciprofloxacin." When he left the room I searched the Internet and had some questions when he got back.

"Doc, *Time* magazine did a cover story on ciprofloxacin during the anthrax scare. They claimed doxycycline works better, but pharmaceutical companies make much more money from ciprofloxacin."

"You'll be fine," he insisted. "You just need some fresh air. Take some time off."

Six years of medical school to tell me I need fresh air? He could be a quack. I googled him—and used *Visine.* Then I cheered up realizing that although I had a swollen testicle, the other one was just fine. I'm an optimist. My sac was half full.

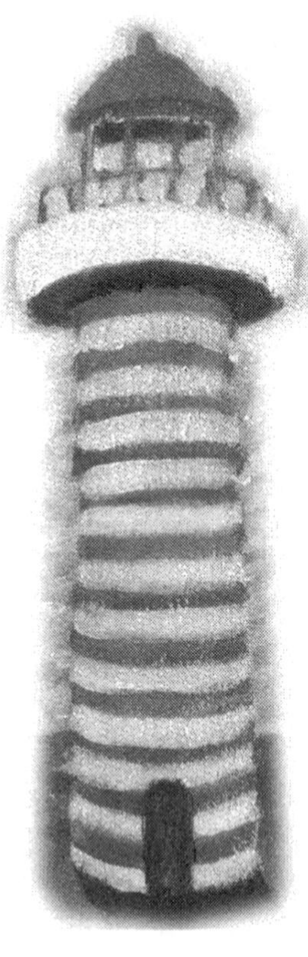

"I am too alone in the world,
and not alone enough
to make every minute holy.
I am too tiny in this world, and
not tiny enough
just to lie before you like a thing,
shrewd and secretive.
I want my own will, and I want
simply to be with my will,
as it goes toward action,
and in the silent, sometimes
hardly moving times
when something is coming
nearer,
I want to be with those who
know secret things
or else alone...
I want to unfold.
I don't want to stay folded
anywhere,
because where I am folded,
there I am a lie...."

Rainer Maria Rilke,
translation by Robert
Bly, "I Am Too Alone in
the World"

The One

"I think I know you," said the woman next to me.

"Yeah, I'm always mistaken for Clooney," I replied.

"Rosemary?" she asked.

We both laughed, and then I recognized her: Dana Williams! We laughed like we did when we were in love fifteen years ago, back when she lived in Seattle and I lived in Hollywood. After five months, she cooled off. I pursued her with long handwritten letters and phone calls. Soon, she asked me never to call her again.

And here we were, meeting this time while I was performing stand-up on a cruise ship. We hung out for three wonderful, platonic days.

But I was in love. On the second day she wondered, "Why do you think we met up again?" I was thinking, "Because you're my soul mate and we're getting a second chance!" But I replied, "Maybe for closure." Closure? What the hell did I say that for? I didn't want closure. This was my chance to have that lifelong romance that has always eluded me. So I continued, "Or maybe for a new beginning, maybe so I can understand what I really want in a relationship."

When we parted, she said, "Paul, you are wonderful, incredible." I replied, "You're wonderful and incredible, too, Dana. She seemed taken aback and said, "Let me leave now before I cry."

Now Dana lived in Maui; I was in Santa Monica. The way her light, sky blue eyes took me in put me at such ease, even though from the moment I saw her again I was tormented. I didn't want to blow it this time.

In other relationships, I've been the interim boyfriend. Boy meets Girl. Boy loses Girl. Girl dates me for six months, then Boy gets Girl back. I was a love temp and happy about it. Red flags turned me on; they gave me an exit strategy. One first date told me she had cancer and her doctor gave her six months to live. I thought to myself, "She's perfect."

That all changed six years ago when I experienced my mom's slow death. It was devastating and profound. It showed me the beauty and necessity of pain. The severe distress expressed the deep love we shared. After she died, I was willing to stop avoiding pain. I was willing to be devastated. No more Steve Buscemi. I was ready to be George Clooney!

For five months after meeting up again, Dana and I stayed in touch with amusing emails and phone calls. She had recently ended a long-term relationship, and emailed: "Life is funny. After my first child, it was so painful I said, 'Never again.' Then time goes by, and you think, I would like another one of those critters. Same with relationships, you break up and think 'never again,' then time goes by..."

At the end of a phone call, she said, "Paul, I don't know how else to say this: I love you." Then she talked about a soul connection between us that must have started before this lifetime. "And I will definitely meet you again in the afterlife," she said. I added, "I hope we see each other before then."

I got myself booked on a cruise ship to Maui. We would have three more days together—three days to find out if we had a friendship, a romance, or just a spiritual reunion in the afterlife. A friend warned me, "You might want to pursue a woman who never said, 'Don't ever call me again.'"

We arranged to meet under the Banyan Tree in Lahaina. I labored over what to wear. My swanky Sinatra hat screamed, "Choose me." I wore it and felt self-conscious.

"Well, this is bizarre," she said when we met up. Bizarre? How about amazing? She looked ravishing, wearing a simple, sexy, black dress. Romance! We hugged. She was stiff.

Friendship!

We had a lovely dinner, listened to luau music, and gazed out on the sparkling sea and the volcanoes that formed Maui. She mentioned that she occasionally gets washed over with an out-of-body type of euphoria and it was happening that night while we were watching the sunset.

After four hours, we parted. "Well, I haven't talked this much in a long time," she said. Romance! We hugged and I kissed her pursed lips, a quick peck. Friendship! I could feel the tension between us and wanted to say that whether we ended up friends or lovers, it was great to have her back in my life. But that would have been a lie: I wanted to star in this movie.

The next night before dinner we drove to a spectacular cliff to view another sunset. A perfect place for a kiss. I stood by her side, my arms stiff. A painful place not to kiss.

However, things changed after dinner: she gave me a kiss that was passionate and loud. Progress! But as I processed it, I realized it was a smooch, a muaaaaaaaa! The kind you get from your grandma. As if she was going to give me a quarter and send me on an errand.

The enthusiasm I loved about Dana was missing. The conversations were fine, but touched on nothing about what was or wasn't going on between us. We were two frightened people who kept meeting up for dinner.

The next day she told me she woke up with a voice telling her "no!" She had to trust her intuition. How could I argue with that? She wanted me, but God had other plans. And she felt my perfect match was just around the corner. Rejection hurts—it's worse with a referral.

Ironically, I got closure. It was great to see how far I had come. Fifteen years ago, I felt unlovable; this time, I knew it wasn't personal. She loved me, just not in my current incarnation.

Two weeks after my return from Maui, I literally walked around the corner from my house into an art gallery and met Emma. Something about her green eyes and ruby lips made me want to dance. So I did. She smiled and asked me out for coffee. I said, "No way. You deserve a whole meal."

With Emma, there is an attraction but not an obsession—a willingness to be revealed, not a longing to be saved.

There is a love that tells me not to hide any part of myself.

For over a year I've been George Clooney.

Three months after I met Emma, she recalled how she helped her son, D.J., when he was five years old and about to have braces put on his misaligned legs. D.J. was very fond of Danny, his cowboy doll. So Emma had a matching pair of braces put on Danny weeks before D.J. was to receive his. All the kids in D.J.'s kindergarten class thought Danny was so cool.

After D.J. got his new braces he strutted into class all smiles, ready for adventure. D.J. and Danny were a big hit. They went everywhere together.

When I heard that story I knew I was officially in love with Emma.

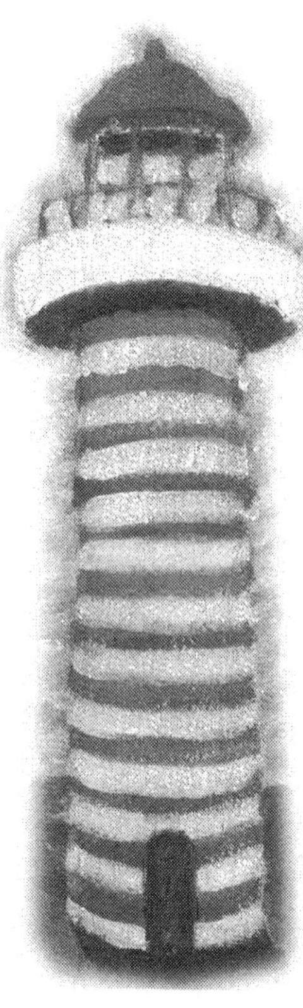

"Our deepest fear is not that we
are inadequate.
Our deepest fear is that we are
powerful beyond measure.
It is our light, not our darkness
that most frightens us.
We ask ourselves, Who am I to
be brilliant, gorgeous, talented,
fabulous?
Actually who are you not to be?
You are a child of God. Your
playing small does not serve the
world.
There is nothing enlightened
about shrinking so that other
people won't feel insecure
around you.
We are all meant to shine, as
children do.
We were born to make manifest
the glory of God that is within
us. It's not just in some of us; it's
in everyone.
And as we let our own light
shine, we unconsciously give
other people permission to do
the same.
As we are liberated from our
own fear, our presence
automatically liberates others."

Marianne Williamson

Pop Was No Weasel

My dad reads every medical journal there is; he's chock full of information. The other day he said, "Paul, most strokes happen on the toilet." "What am I supposed to do with that information?" I thought. Well, it's a good thing I have a backyard.

My dad and I get along great now, but for a long while I carried resentment about something he said to me when I was eleven: "Wake up, you'll never amount to anything."

I had failed to sweep the floor properly. My dad had a janitorial job at night, and he'd taken his sons to help out. I remember thinking at the time, "I will not end up doing this grunt work. I will never be like you."

For years, I've worked at being nothing like him. Now, I'd like to be more like him. He knows how to have fun. Rarely do I permit myself to enjoy a movie or a ballgame without a nagging sense that I should be doing something productive. I always feel like I'm falling behind. Sunsets stand for disappointment, showing me that the day is over and I haven't gotten enough done.

In the 1990s, the rage was getting in touch with your inner child. I went back to the building where I used to help my dad clean. As I stood there looking through a window, I realized that I was the one who had been so hard on myself and hard on my dad. For twenty years

I'd made him wrong. I always wanted an apology from him, I owed myself an apology.

I had made myself approach each day as if I had to prove something. I was living my life as if the man who had given me so much support was my nemesis. Well, I have met the enemy and it's me.

Since that day at the window, I've acquired a lot more respect for my dad. And rightfully so. I now see him as a Bobby Knight, a guy with intensity who sometimes went too far, but only because of his passion for life. I see the humor of his yelling at the top of his lungs for me to "relax." And as I get older, my appreciation for him keeps growing. I find that the more esteem I have for my dad, the more esteem I have for myself—and the more acceptance I can have for my own humanity, with all the anger, frustration, and mistakes.

As a mail carrier and a janitor my dad provided for a family of nine. Wow! I just manage to provide for myself, a party of one.

I may not feel I accomplished enough today—I rarely do—but I don't want that to be a reason not to seek joy, not to believe everything is happening just as it should be. I'm right here for me; I always will be. I've turned a life of insecurity and negativity into one of genuine gratitude and understanding.

I've also come to appreciate the little things, like going to the bathroom. I used to look at it as an interruption. But now, when I have a bowel movement it makes my day. I'm on the throne five minutes ahead of time and I celebrate afterwards. I call home: "Hey, Pop, it's Paul. I'm regular. And I didn't have a stroke."

We are what we see in others.

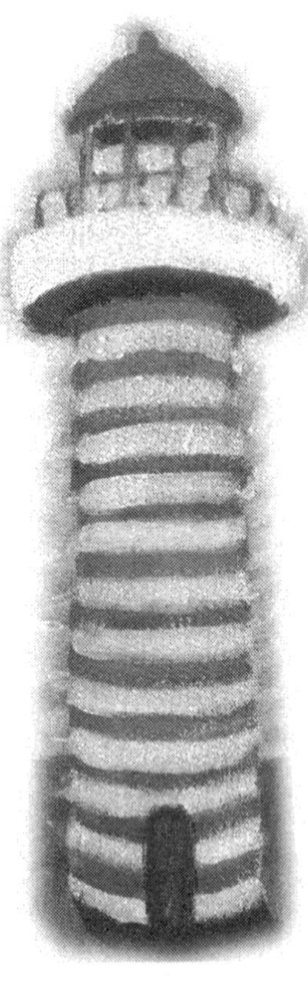

"I have found it of enormous value when I can permit myself to understand another person. Our first reaction to most other people is an immediate evaluation, or judgment, rather than an understanding of it. When someone expresses some feeling or attitude or belief, our tendency is to feel 'That's right' or 'that's stupid." Very rarely do we permit ourselves to understand precisely the meaning of their statement. I believe this is because understanding is risky. If I let myself really understand another person, I might be changed by that understanding. And we all fear change."

Carl Rogers

Game Changer

I'm subjected to prejudice daily because of my condition: aging. After jogging yesterday I leaned over to catch my breath, like I've done for the last forty years. A car swerved to the side of the road and a young dude asked if I was okay. "Okay? Am I okay? Best shape of my life, you little fetus. I just ran three miles. Get lost. Go to Calcutta and feed the hungry, you no good Samaritan!" I would have yelled some more, but my left arm started feeling numb. Why didn't he give me credit for jogging? Well, I call it jogging even though today I was passed by, by a woman with a walker. But let's be fair— she got extra bounce from the tennis balls.

My own age-based prejudice raised its ugly head several years ago. I was forty-seven years old talking to a colleague, Joe. He was fifty-one and said, "You and me, you know, we're the same age." I thought, "No way! I am not your age! I'm in my forties; you're in your fifties. I could get another college degree by the time I reach your age. I could visit every country in the world. I could have four kids and one on the way."

Another age-based indignity occurred recently during a game of pick-up basketball with guys in their twenties. After playing for fifteen minutes no one had passed me the ball. I was wide open. No one was guarding me. They were thinking, "He's old; he can't shoot." How dare they! I can shoot. I've got game.

Then I caught myself. I made a positive pivot and committed to being the happiest player on the court. It's not whether I get to shoot, win or lose, but did I enjoy the game? I play basketball to have fun, to move, to get in shape. What good is it to get all bent out of shape? Look at what I can do. I can play defense. I can get a rebound. I can steal the ball— from my own teammate! I am the master of my mirth. I am the boss of my ball-playing bliss.

Recently, I joined a league for guys over fifty. Most of the players are over sixty. They call me kid. We spend more time getting dressed for the game then playing the game: put on an ankle brace, pop an Advil; put on kneepads, pop an Advil; wrap on a back supporter, pop an Advil—and a Claritan in case somebody opens a window. We walk out looking like mummies. Our games vaguely resemble basketball. We scour the court with the same agility that the old electric football players displayed when you plugged the game in. We all end up stuck in a corner wiggling. But it is very exciting to watch guys over fifty play basketball. Everyone is on the edge of their seats hoping we make it—up the court.

I was upset the other day because I didn't start, even though I consider myself one of the top three players. I went back into my "poor me" routine. Again I caught myself and said, "Paul calm down, you can handle this!

Look at what you can do." So I had fun from the bench. I cheered the guys on and it worked: the additional exertion caused one of the guys to get angina.

As I focus on joy and see how I sometimes lose sight of it, what I regret is letting results and expectations matter more than my own happiness. Many guys are miserable when they play because they only focus on winning. After I missed a lay-up one teammate, shouted, "You've got to make those!" Oh, really? Is that the idea? To get the ball through the hoop? Wow, you learn something new every day.

After I missed my lay-up the other team scored and won. They were celebrating, and I rejoiced with them. Let's face it: they couldn't have done it without me.

Winning is for losers, too.

"It's a sad day when you find out that it's not accident or fortune but just yourself that kept things from you."

Lillian Hellman

Laughing in Laughlin

In Laughlin, Nevada, five large casinos have sprouted along the Colorado River. The town is a giant nursing home; its rehab machines are known as slots. The average age is deceased. That's just a rough estimate. I love it there. Everyone calls me kid!

The bare, rolling mountains and desert crevices mimic the wrinkled faces of all the octogenarian smokers. Many of them remember the mountains when they were molehills. There's a certain beauty to the old smokers' wrinkled skin; it no longer fits their faces (the skin is a large, the face a small). They could peel off their faces and reveal themselves as Scooby-Doo villains.

I walk the streets in constant peril of being attacked by a menacing gang in town, the Red Hat Ladies. Their rule is no rules. They offer each other support and give themselves per- mission to be crazy. After years of self-conscious normality, they parade around like purple peacocks.

This is a man's world, but at sixty the women take over. Shunning the conventions that once stymied their spontaneity, they're free at last. Women, on average, live ten years longer than men, who can expect to die at seventy-one. Not me. When I turn seventy, I'm moving to Laughlin, getting a sex change, and joining the Red Hat Ladies. And I'll start smoking.

My good friends Mark and Jennifer Restine, who were visiting the ghost towns along Route 66, stopped by. They'd gotten a flat tire the day before. Mark was ecstatic: "The mechanic told us stories for two hours." Vacations are wonderful, even getting a flat tire can be an adventure: "Wow, we got to meet the mechanic!" On my next trip to the ER, I'll get to meet a doctor.

Mark was amazed by the green cactus trees bursting into an orange blaze at sunset. It's amazing what happens when we slow down and take the world in. His outlook had an effect on me. I'd been anxious about writing something that afternoon. So I stopped and took things in: the silence, the wind, a boat drifting by. Wow!

I applied that same attitude when I performed that night. The audience was great, but I wasn't feeling "with it." I decided to take the focus off of me and take the audience in. I saw an eighty-four-year-old woman sitting up front. She seemed to be asleep. At least I hoped she was asleep. The sound guy played music and she came back to life like in Awakenings.

While I was talking onstage about the health benefits of having a dog, a woman in the audience shouted out, "I don't want a dog."

"People with dogs live five years longer," I told her.

"I want to come and go as I please!" she screamed.

"Well, it's tough to come and go when you're dead."

The secret of life is taking it in, not taking it over. Carpe diem mañana!

I have ADHD, but I look at it this way:

I'm a multi-tasker!

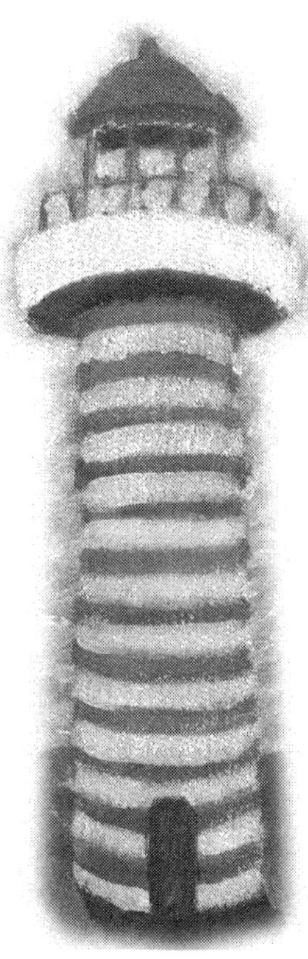

"Anyone on the spiritual path who falls upon hard times should not turn to that friend who encourages their old self to survive. Rather they can seek out someone who will faithfully and inexorably help them to risk themselves, so that they may endure the suffering and pass courageously through it. Only to the extent that we expose our self to annihilation, can that which is indestructible arise within us. In this lies the dignity of daring."

From *The Way of Transformation*, by Karlfried Graf Dürckheim

Knocking on Heaven's Door

When my mom was dying and paralyzed on her right side, I would ask if she wanted to go outside. With a smirk she'd raise her only moveable limb, her right arm, point her finger, and say, "Let's go." There was so little she could do outside. But after a few minutes, she'd smile and say, "Hear the birds?"

It's the little victories that count. I overlook so much— my daily concerns and desires drowning out the moments of delight, sounds, sights, and sensations. I am rarely fully present to life.

I enjoy Leviticus, my cat. Her silky fur, her purring, and the way she falls over on her side in sheer abandon to receive a massage. When I was first told Mom had a brain tumor the size of a golf ball, I put down the phone and Leviticus sat next to me. All the times I absent-mindedly petted her seemed like mere practice for this moment. I wanted so much to experience this petting, this moment with Leviticus, to enjoy giving her pleasure.

My life as I'd known it was crumbling. I always knew I would lose my mom someday. She was a smoker since fourteen. Dad would watch her smoke and say, "Those cigarettes are going to kill ya." She would exhale the smoke, twist out the cigarette, smirk, and say, "Well, that one didn't."

Now Mom's someday was close at hand. It felt so good to touch Leviticus, to experience the flow of my fingers through her slippery multicolored fur coat. Leviticus's few pounds of flesh, savoring my touch, purring with delight, unaware of death, comforted me. I remembered my dad's frequent phrase, "We are only passing through." It hadn't really meant anything to me before. But now its matter-of-fact truth gave me solace. No one gets out of here alive. Every day is a gift. The ultimate paradox: it is death that gives life its precious meaning.

For the next three years I watched my mom slowly die, but mostly I watched her awaken. The first year she was filled with irritation at the continuing assault of her non-Hodgkin's lymphoma, the humiliations and her limitations. At the end of the first year she got to a point where she accepted all of it. She cared less and less about the indignity of having some- one bathe her. Instead she was grateful, saying thank you for every little thing anyone did. Her gratitude was amazing.

Mom was quick to laugh. One time when I was visiting her at the nursing home, her devoted, loving, gregarious aide, Helen was telling Mom about a dinner she had prepared and went into every detail about it. A woman in the corner, Mary, piped in, "Helen, watch your arm." Helen looked at one arm, then the other.

"Which arm?" she asked. Mary cocked her head: "The arm that's patting yourself on the back." Mom and Helen both cracked up.

At the nursing home, one woman, Anne, was constantly calling for help during meals, and the aides started to ignore her. One day when no help came, Anne got up, walked to the middle of the dining hall, lifted her skirt, and proceeded to do the whole works on the floor. "There now," she asked sweetly, "who's going to help me?" Mom and Helen broke out in uncontrollable laughter, and Helen said, "Wow, I could have peed myself." Mom replied, "I just did."

The end of dignity is the beginning of freedom.

We overlook so much every day. All the little things people do for us: a call to say hello, greetings from strangers, someone making you smile or a driver waving you on to pull in front of them. (Whenever this happens, I get out of my car and hug them.)

Mom focused less on what she used to be able to do and more and more on what she could do and see in the present. She accepted her death, welcomed her death, but she didn't resign herself to it. She lived fully. Her faith and life-long Catholic beliefs were put to the test. Mom just put her life in God's hands and lived with love. She looked forward to heaven, to seeing her parents, brothers, and sister, and to whatever else this next adventure might bring.

It's the most meaningful lesson and profound gift parents can share with their children—how to die. To see Mom let go and awaken, to see her so broken down, yet whole. I wake up now and wonder how often I can say "thank you."

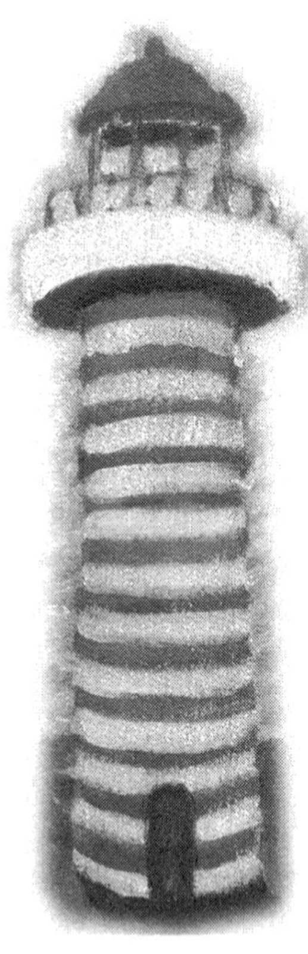

"There is a vitality, a life force, a quickening that is translated through you into action, and because there is only one of you in all of time, this expression is unique. And if you block it, it will never exist through any other medium and it will be lost. The world will not have it.
It is not your business to determine how good it is, nor how valuable it is. It is your business to keep it yours clearly and directly, to keep the channel open. You do not even have to believe in yourself or your work. You have to keep open and aware to the urges that motivate you. Keep the channel open. No artist is pleased. . . . There is only a queer, divine dissatisfaction, a blessed unrest that keeps us marching and makes us more alive."

Martha Graham

Fool for Love

Thanks to online dating, I've quadrupled my rate of rejection. Dating was getting expensive. I went from having dinners to coffee dates where I'd show up ten minutes late so she'd already have her drink. If the date was going well, I paid for a refill. I'm a fool for love.

One woman I dated was trying to size up my financial empire before deciding if I was worthy of a kiss. She wanted to know if I owned my apartment. I rent a 400-square-foot studio. Still snooping, she asked me if my apartment was a one bedroom or two. I said, "Keep going, but not up."

I live simply. For the most part, I have achieved my teenage dream of never having an alarm clock wake me up. But I haven't achieved the second half of that dream: having my sweetheart wake me up around noon. I fulfilled my dream of no alarm clock, but with no one around to wake me up. Why? I have a lot to offer a woman—like section 8 housing. What's wrong? It shouldn't be this hard.

I felt the need to step it up, get a bigger place, make more money. Most women in their fifties like to travel without using friends' couches. Then I met Emma. When she first saw my apartment, she said, "Wow, we have the same taste." She looked at the books on my shelf: The Prophet and Green Eggs and Ham.

"Of course," she said, "two of my favorite books." At her apartment, I told her she had my favorite quote up on her wall, the one that includes the line: "We were born to shine the way children do." She said, "Of course."

On our second date, I told her, "I like the way you kiss."
She said, "I like the way we kiss." Wow. We!

On our third date, we crashed a wedding reception and danced. Rarely have I met someone who danced like me, with abandon and joy, like a Holy Roller receiving the Holy Ghost. She watched me dance and said, "Of course." We even got applause. I was soon asking myself, What's wrong? It shouldn't be this easy.

She said, "We are going to have so much fun together." Wow, she didn't say, "Let's get serious"! She said we are going to have fun. How perfect.

After three months, we were saying things like, "I really, really like you." We were running out of adjectives. "I like you so, so much, so enormously. You are super-duper. You are the cat's meow. You are the pelican's pouch." So one night I said it: "Emma, I love you." She whispered back, "I know." I know? Oh, no! My thoughts raced: maybe she just wants to have fun! I got too heavy! Maybe she just really, really likes me! Then I saw tears running down her cheeks. She said, "Paul, those words never meant so much to me." I went back to breathing and thought, "Of course."

A month later, she told me, "I will never forget the first time you said 'I love you.'" I said, "I am never going to forget the first time you said 'I know.'"

I love it when a woman *whispers in my ear* when we're being romantic. When she says,

"Oh, Paul… oh, oh… Ohhhhh Paul!"

I love that, when she gets my name right.

"In the middle of difficulty lies opportunity."

Albert Einstein

Passport to Happiness

I whisk past the long maze of miserable people meandering through the American Airlines ticketing area and glide up to the first class counter ready to be pampered. I've earned this VIP status because of all the miles I fly when I'm performing on cruise ships, in casinos, and at the occasional Purim celebration. I hand the agent my passport. She examines it and begins typing furiously without looking up. Finally she speaks: "You can't fly with this." I tell her I know; that's why I'm getting on a plane. She is not amused. "This is mutilated," she says. Hundreds of people have seen my passport this year; no one ever warned me it was getting too worn. Not just worn, but mutilated. Like I'm guilty of vio- lating my passport. This poor woman is going to get fired.

"Can we have a manager look at that?" I ask, trying not to be too VIP condescending to the woman on her last day at work. The manager comes over and agrees with the employee, then another manager arrives and agrees with both of them. Well, it looks like American Airlines will have job openings tomorrow.

She shows me where the back passport cover has a split. (Obviously the work of Al Qaeda.) I offer to glue it.

"That would be tampering with your passport."

I am not happy. I call the cruise line and learn that my ship won't be leaving port till tomorrow. Great. All I need is a new passport—today!

I call the U.S. passport agency and get a live person. Amazing! My tax dollars at work. I tell him I need an appointment. "No problem," he says. Wow, life has a way of working out. Then he says he'll transfer me over to the automated appointment system. So they employ live people to direct callers to an automated line. No wonder I cheat on my taxes. The next available appointment is five days away, so I decide to drive over to the passport agency; after all, 80 percent of success is showing up. A security guard tells me you must have an appointment, then listens to my plight and lets me through.

Once I'm inside, the agent says my passport will be ready that day. Wow, America! And to top it all off I have a free evening to enjoy before shipping out. A few hours later, I meet some friends for happy hour (actually three hours of happy at half price.) Afterwards, we catch a buddy of ours playing music at my favorite honky-tonk bar. The bass player cracks me up with this anecdote: "When I was home I was giving my dog a bath—and that's not a euphemism. I dried him off with a towel and then after my own bath realized it was the only towel I had. So I'm clean, but I smell like a Labradoodle."

What a great night! I'm lucky my passport was denied. I am so quick to assume a change in plans is awful. I must remember to send that woman at the airport flowers.

I'm learning Tai Chi in case I get attacked by a very lethargic mugger.

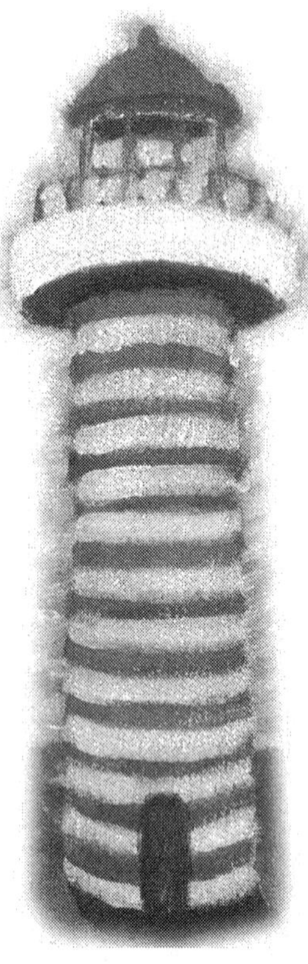

"When you pass through
anger and self deprecation
and have the strength to
acknowledge it all

When the past makes you
laugh
and you can savor the magic
that let you survive your own
war

You find that that fire is
passion
and there's a door up ahead
not a wall"
Lou Reed

Throwing My Weight Around

The moment you make a decision, you change your life," says Tony Robbins. I make decisions, but the only thing that changes is my mind. The decisions are constantly being appealed and overturned.

Two months ago, after reaching a peak in overweightness, I vowed to start a diet soon. Then I began to gorge, eating everything I was about to be deprived of. What happened? My decision accomplished the opposite of what I intended. My weight peak, it turned out, was only a plateau.

I started giving myself positive thoughts: "Hey, Paul, you're not as fat as that guy . . . or that guy . . . or that guy." I didn't need to diet. I needed to go to Walmart, look around, and appreciate my restraint.

I'd stopped being self-critical, but I still wasn't eating in a way that brought joy. I was resigned to being plump and sluggish. Then, for a few days, I forgot to eat late at night and woke up feeling much better. Lighter. I liked it. Suddenly, it became more important for me to feel good in the morning than to eat apple pie at 2 a.m. I made a positive pivot.

I don't feel deprived at all now. My urges don't have the best of me. My desire to feel good when I wake up is usually stronger than having that late-night apple strudel. Carpe diem, mañana. I know when I do give in. It's a momentary lapse. And I make sure I enjoy it.

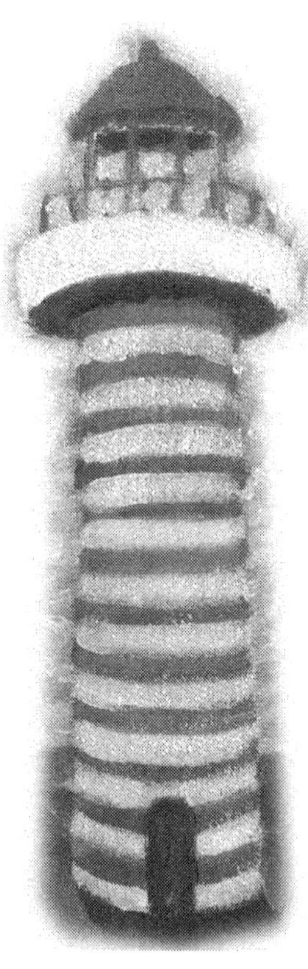

"The curious paradox is that when I accept myself as I am, then I change. We cannot change, we cannot move away from what we are, until we thoroughly accept what we are. Then change seems to come about unnoticed."

Carl Rogers

How to Help the Homeless

The *Bed, Bath and Beyond* coupons keep arriving. It's alpha mail. I can't get enough. I live in a big old house divided into apartments. Our mailboxes are not secure, just tin boxes on the porch. No keys, just old-fashioned American trust. So when the coupons arrive I pluck them all.

Last week my neighbor, Hank got a fresh issue of the *New Yorker.* Or to be precise I got it. It's great fun, that New Yorker. The cartoons are even funnier when you're not paying that steep subscription. I love free. In my kitchen I horde tiny half-and-half creamers that I get at convenience stores. I love complimentary.

I didn't give these proclivities any thought until this morning; as I was getting ready to catch a plane my car was stolen. Someone felt like having it, complimentary. At the police station I told the clerk I'd left the motor running, went upstairs to get my last suitcase, and when I came back the car was gone. She asked, "Did anyone have a spare key?"

I proceeded to recite the facts to her again: The car was running. I started it for them, had it packed and ready to go. Free! She went on with questions that bore no relation to the pure stupidity of leaving a car running, unmanned, and unlocked when you live across the street from a homeless shelter (careless can be very close to car-less). I was about to miss my plane and lose more money.

Somehow, I made it to the airport in time to catch the next flight. On the plane I thumbed through Hank's *New Yorker.* Wow! I suddenly realized how prone I am to thievery. I'd been living a petty life, greedy and unethical. Some guys steal cars; I steal magazines and *Bed, Bath, and Beyond* coupons. I'm a metrosexual bandit. And so cheap, that last month I found a way to save a bundle on my car insurance by taking off comprehensive and theft.

A day after the great heist the police found my car. The thief had gone through my luggage, taken a pair of my shoes and pants, and left me his. In one pocket was a pamphlet for a course he just completed titled "How to Be Self-Employed." I guess the big take-away from that seminar was my car. He also left his paperwork from the homeless shelter. Ethical considerations prevent me from stating his name: Eric Sowell. No grudges, Eric. I understand what it's like to walk in your shoes—literally. I wish you and my pants well. I've always wanted to help the homeless and thought I didn't have enough time. Well, apparently I did.

At home I placed the *New Yorker* and the coupons back in my neighbors' mailboxes. I felt lighter. By 20 percent.

Whenever I get the flu I look at it this way:

I found a way lose five pounds!

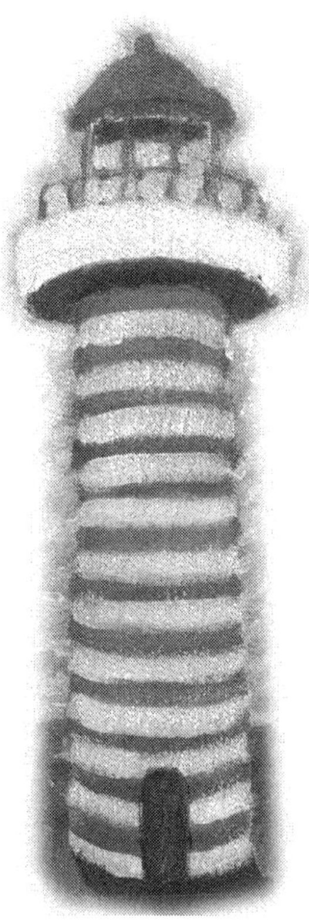

"I will come to you, my friend,
when I no longer need you.
Then you will find a palace,
not an almshouse."
Henry David Thoreau

Me, My Dad, and I Don't Know

For years I blamed my father for my insecurity. If only he gave me more encouragement, if he didn't yell so much. When I was thirty-six it dawned on me. I had been out of the house for eighteen years. Maybe daddy wasn't the problem. I had to admit the truth: Mom screwed up.

I'm noticing a common thread. When I'm in a relationship, I'm miserable and then when I'm single, I'm miserable. I'm starting to figure out who the problem is: all I have to do is get rid of me and I'll have the life I've always dreamed of. Wouldn't it be great if we could divorce ourselves, start all over?

"Hey Paul."

"Oh, I'm not Paul—we split up. Nothing was ever good enough for him."

"You're right, you are better off. He was a judgmental jerk."

"Hey, easy. It's tough not to take that personally."

Experts say we can't have good relationships with others until we love ourselves. So I've been working on my relationship with myself. And it's really working out. It's the little things I do. The surprises. I walk into the bathroom and there's a Post-it on the mirror: "I'm so lucky to be you." Wow, that's so thoughtful. On my headboard there's a note: "You're the best I ever had." Wow, I think I could be the one. I just finished balancing my checkbook— time for another note: Paul is solvent and sexy! I was on the corner today. A lot of people thought I was cold. I was just cuddling. Quality time with Paul.

I am finally giving myself the attention I need. For years everyone listened to my advice—except me. Now I know better. Still, I question my own authority. Who am I to tell me what to do? I've worked on myself for years, never realizing that any image I have of myself is simply that--an image, an illusion. Each day now I set out to discover who I am rather than presuming who I am. I am living with much less certainty and more "I don't know."

It is my certainty about who I am and who my dad is that really gets in my way. We are all so much more than we think we are. I don't need to improve. I just need to let go of any image I have of myself, of the ideal of who I think I should be. To be continually new and fresh, that is my intention. Perhaps someday I will get to the point where I can say I am not the same person I was when I began this sentence.

If you want joy in your life, you've got to get a dog. They always cheer you up. After a horrible day, people cutting you off in traffic, boss breathing down you neck, creditors sending you pink envelopes. As soon as you think, "Life sucks! Nobody cares!" All you have to do is step on your sidewalk and your dog goes crazy,

"Omg! Omg! It's you, it's you, I care! I care. Let me get you a toy! Every day you leave and then you come back! I love you!"

If you have a cat and you come home he's like,

"Oh it's you again. If you swept the floor I wouldn't have to clean myself every two seconds!"

But with a dog it's a Broadway show,

"It's the greatest person in the world!"

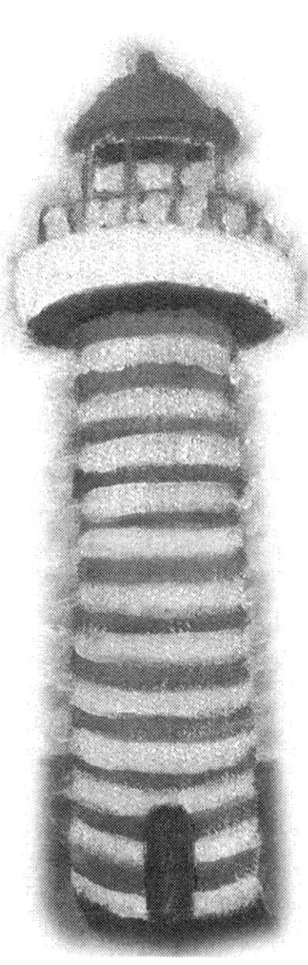

"Only when we understand the true relationship between each other is there a possibility of love, and love is denied when we have images. Therefore it is important to understand, not intellectually but actually in your daily life, how you have built images about your wife, your husband, your neighbor, your child, your country, your leaders, your gods—you have nothing but images."

Jiddu Krisnamurti

How to Hula

Maui is beautiful, palm trees swaying, warm air mingling with the cool breeze. I'm soaking up the local color, sitting outside a lovely cafe the natives call Starbucks reading a book I purchased from a store they call Barnes and Noble. Maybe I'll eat at the local bistro, Applebees. Ah, Hawaii!

I promised myself I would get back to writing; I've been putting it off all day. I just spent eight days at home in Santa Monica not writing, not working at all. Carpe diem mañana. As usual, I'm torn between fun and productivity. Two teenage boys are talking loudly at the next table, pants low, baseball caps sideways, giggling. Possibly stoned. One wears a shirt that reads, "Welcome to Hawaii, now get lost." An older Hispanic guy walks up and says hello; they do an elaborate handshake. Gangbangers? The older guy's arm is littered with tattoos. He asks, "You guys on for basketball tonight?" They were. I love the game so I ask where they're playing. "At our church. We're Mormons."

Of course! My assumptions are so often negative and flat-out wrong. These Latter Day Godbangers ask me to join them. They're having a luau, which along with the traditional grilling and dancing includes playing basketball. Wow, I guess you could call it a Luau Cinder, or a Kareem Abdul Jabarbeque.

But I was hoping to write tonight. Should I stay or should I go? I'm so lazy. I'm reminded of the time I was eleven on my way to play basketball. My dad said, "Basketball ain't import- ant; get the weeds." I hated pulling weeds. Worse, I hated not having a say in the matter. I hated my dad, so tyrannical. He'd labeled me lazy and tried to instill a work ethic in me. So I pulled the weeds growing under the pricker bush and cursed everything; the thorns and my life.

Debating whether to play ball or write, I remembered something I read by Henry David Thoreau: before we can write we need to have a life worth writing about. So I venture out to experience Maui. This is the time to take it all in: waterfalls and volcanoes, luaus and basketball, Macy's and Foot Locker.

Along the way I laugh at how I thought the young Mormons were thugs. And I realize I'd formed a similar wrong conclusion about my dad. As long as I held him as a tyrant I couldn't, wouldn't speak up to him, to ask him if it would be okay to pull the weeds after I played ball.

I keep walking. I know I'm in the Mormon area when I pass several small "Mom, Mom, Mom and Pop" shops. I arrive at the church and immediately get to play. On the bench a young guy strums a ukulele. Here I am, having a genuine Hawaiian experience.

Afterwards I join the other church members and learn a few hula moves. Every gesture means something, like sign language. Thanking God for the sun you put your arms high in the air; thanking God for the waves you wiggle your arms from side to side.

The physical activity of playing basketball and dancing awakened my body and brought me out of my head. I walked back to the ship ready to pull some weeds.

"I cherish my wounds and
their cures
and the sweet enervations of
bliss
My book is an open life

I wave goodbye to the
absolutes
and send my regards to infinity
I'd rather be blithe than
correct

Until something transcendent
turns up
I splash in my poetry puddle
and try to keep God amused."

James Broughton,
"Having Come This Far"

Carma

I dread this moment: buying a car. I'm impulsive and trusting. Car dealers love me. I found out that when a salesman says, "we'll throw in a bumper-to-bumper warranty," he doesn't mean for free. And do bumpers need coverage? A 2000 Jeep was posted on Craigslist for $4,000, much cheaper than a dealership scam. "It runs great," said Rosa, whom I trusted immediately. I sensed her wholesomeness and generosity; she didn't wear make-up or a bra. "Oil's dirty, needs a change, that's all," she said. I appreciated her candor.

"I'll bring cash tomorrow." Rosa wasn't comfortable with cash. It could be counterfeit. She wanted a money order, I suppose a non-counterfeit money order.

"Take it to a mechanic," my paranoid brother Chris insisted. "It runs great," I said. It's only been driven by Rosa and her mom. Needs an oil change, that's all." I was too embarrassed to admit I was in a rush and didn't even test drive it. I trusted Rosa. Chris insisted. I obliged.

I met Rosa the next day at a dealership that was willing to check the car and change the oil for $32. A great deal. My friend drove. "Just drop me off, Ron. I'll be driving home." Ron stayed and chatted with Rosa, who he trusted immediately. The inspection was thorough and the manager was upfront. They found six leaks. Six holes? Did she lend it to Bonnie and Clyde?

Didn't Rosa know? Where did she think all that oil on her driveway was coming from? The Gulf? It would cost $1,700 to fix. Ron, with a crush on Rosa, informed us that he knew a mechanic who could fix everything for $400. I quickly added, "But the mechanic's in prison."

Rosa suggested that the leaks might not be that much of a problem; perhaps they didn't even have to be fixed, since you could just keep filling the tanks up to just below the holes. Seriously? And maybe we could seal the holes with Bubblicious? It dawned on me that I might have been too trusting.

Rosa wouldn't budge on price. "I can't sell it for less," she said. "I need the $4,000 towards my new car."

Good luck with that. Rosa wasn't selling the car for what it was worth; she was selling it for how much she needed. Her Jeep was a counterfeit! I wanted to trust her; she wanted to believe her car was running great. Who needs reality? I got the bill and told Rosa I had paid for the oil change thinking she'd contribute something. She did: a hearty "thanks!"

Next time I'm hiring a mechanic, a psychologist and not bringing a friend who is so easily smitten. Buying a car should be more like dating, more of a drawn-out process. I can't believe I got so close to going all the way with a Jeep on a first date. I need to buy a car from someone I can really trust. I'm getting a good vibe about that dealership.

People who have pets live five years longer! So, those ladies with 40 cats, they are not crazy. They have been around since Lincoln.

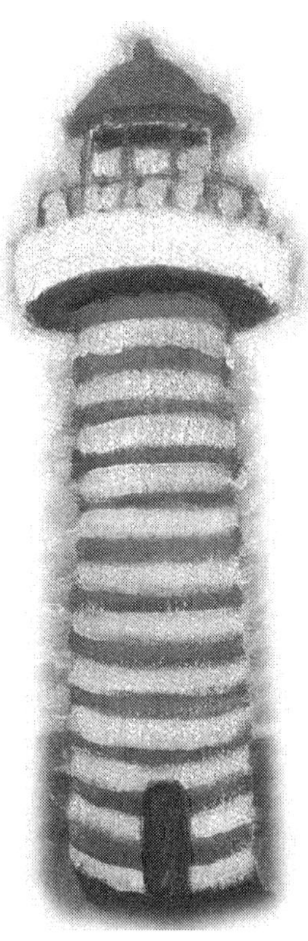

"Attention is the rarest and
purest form of generosity."
Simone Weil

Intimacy for Dummies

Emma lives on a mountaintop in Topanga Canyon, California, in a refurbished mobile home the interior of which begs to be photographed for Better Homes and Trailers. She has transformed a dark and depressing rattrap into an ode to joy. Underneath the clear glaze on her kitchen counter are shellacked poems like: "She said she usually cried at least once a day not because she was sad, but because the world was so beautiful and life was so short."

Emma sleeps beside her trailer in a tent with a large chandelier over her teak bed. To see the stars she slides the bed out onto her deck. How could I not fall in love with her?

After our first few dates, Emma nonchalantly said, "I'm low maintenance." This woman was so free she seemed like no maintenance. However, in our twelve months together, we've broken down two dozen times and broken up six times. The most nonchalant couple in the world has become quite chalant. And since we are both committed to spiritual growth, we love it. (Okay, we accept it. Who really sees a problem in a relationship and says, "Oh great, a growth opportunity!"?)

We get along great when we're together, but I travel a bit. Emma would say a lot. When I am in town, we hang out a lot—she would say a bit. The demons often arise when I go away. On one occasion, we had a designated calling time that came and went. Later Emma said, "I lost my phone, so I figured that was a sign we weren't meant to talk." Why didn't it mean you were meant to look for your phone?" I thought.

Emma is an artist. Her paintings are colorful abstract emotional landscapes. She's all heart. I'm all intellect. She says I think too much, and I have given that a lot of thought. I've come to realize her way is not wrong; it's simply how she navigates the world. Still, my lifestyle sends her emotions all over the place, and her moods send my thoughts all over the place.

We both love freedom, but it means something completely different to each of us. Emma often feels weighed down by my schedule. She loves to treat each day like a blank canvas. I love looking at my calendar—I see all my gigs and all my time off and think, "Yes, the universe is taking care of me!" Emma questions how much I can love her if I enjoy leaving so often. How can she say she loves me if it feels to me like she wants to clip my wings? We both understand the pickle we are in. As much as we do love each other, can we fly together?

On my last trip the problem started with a lie, or more specifically, a withhold. I told Emma I would need to leave for the airport at 7:30 in the morning. But I wanted to leave that early so I could play basketball at the Y before my flight. I didn't want to risk her getting upset that I would pick basketball over her before a long trip. When the morning came, I decided not to play ball after all and instead to spend an extra hour in bed with Emma. I assumed we'd progress from heavy petting to lovemaking because I've got game! Well, she didn't react to my advances because she was thinking we had no time.

I got upset about us not having a little hanky-panky before my ten-day trip—forgetting that I was willing to forego making whoopee to go play basketball in the first place. In our phone call that night (she found her phone), she said, "Oh, I want you so bad right now." I said, "Didn't you want me this morning?" "I guess not," she replied very nonchalantly. So I got upset, but I didn't tell her. I nonchalantly lost interest in the rest of the conversation.

The next day my negative thoughts spiraled. A few days later we were facing a breakup.

When it comes to relationships, Ram Dass said, no one is enlightened. But it seems to me a relationship is the best way to get there. You know you have room to grow when you're having fights over who is more spiritual.

In an intimate relationship you get to enjoy everything that is wonderful about yourself and to understand everything that's not. You learn to navigate as consciously as possible through each other's weakness and beauty. There's no better way to understand yourself.

I didn't want to look at how my "withhold" led to Emma and me having a painful misunderstanding. I wanted to blame her for my upset. So often I blame others for my misery without seeing I am the cause.

I apologized to Emma. And then we made love under the constellations. Because I've got game.

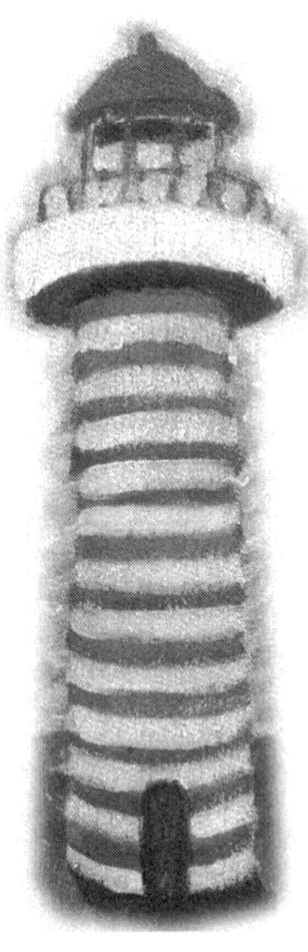

If you want Supreme Reality,
hide from fame.
You're looking for the Pearl?
Plunge, now, to the sea's
bottom.
What's on the shore is only
foam."

Rumi (1207-1273)

Little Victories Are the Vaccines of Life

"Are you sure I need to get the MMR vaccine?" I asked the doctor hopefully, referring to the dreaded mumps, measles, and rabies shot. But I knew the answer. When you work on a cruise ship they want a full physical exam, including drug tests, vaccines, blood work, and some prudent probing.

"Can't the vaccine itself make me ill," I asked. The doctor said it was needed to protect against illnesses from Third World countries. "That's part of the allure of a cruise," I assured him. "You get to meet diseases from all over the world." "That's why you need to be careful," he responded. "You're on a flotilla of bacteria." "Yes," I added, "and all you can eat." I teased him about the hazards of his work and mentioned two words I wouldn't have to worry about: "Staph infections." He smiled and showed me a large needle. Touché.

The shot concluded three weeks of extensive, intensive procedures. A free man with no signs of fever—yet—I jumped in my car, drove to the parking garage exit booth, and said "howdy" to the attendant. For sixty-five minutes parking: twelve dollars. More than my copay. "Cash only," he barked. I only had my credit card, no ATM card, and no cash. Five cars lined up behind me. Then six. Make that seven.

This was humiliating. "Back up, pull into that space, and use the ATM," the attendant demanded. I told him I didn't have my ATM card. He shrugged. I was tempted to crash through the wooden guard bar and take off. The woman in the car directly behind mine, apparently willing to cover for me, was waving money out her window. The attendant walked over and refused it. He asked her to back up. Again she offered him the money and again he turned her down. She backed up. I pulled out of the line and into the designated parking space, figuring I'd call my credit card company to get my pin.

After the woman pulled up and paid her parking, she asked me if she could pay for me. I didn't feel right taking a stranger's twelve dollars. I thanked her and said no. I got my pin, went to the machine, and took out twenty; my credit card company charged me a ten dollar cash advance fee and interest at 23.74 percent. Parking was costing more than my rabies shot. I was rabid!

I wanted to report this ignoramus to the manager. So I called the number on the parking lot wall. The ignoramus answered—he was the manager. "Why didn't you accept her money?" I asked. "Rules," he replied. I started to froth. I wanted to bite this miserable S.O.B., hoping the rabies shot hadn't taken effect. Instead I shouted and called him a stupid ass. He smiled. I pulled out into the sunlight.

I couldn't believe people like him existed. I couldn't stop hating him. I wanted to write the hospital, the newspapers. He is going down! I remembered the woman's sweet gesture. Why does this guy's arrogance pulsate and propel me to action while her sweet gesture dissipates? I thwarted her kindness, embarrassed that I needed the money. I'm so quick to offer help, so reluctant to accept it. I'd rather be incensed than vulnerable, upset rather than grateful. But allowing someone to do a good deed is a good deed in itself. Why not allow myself to be touched? Life is filled with savage indignities; it's salvaged by kindness. As my friend Margie says, "You never regret taking the high road." No you don't. So why didn't he, the stupid ass bastard.

On the way home, seeing my middle shirt button missing and my hairy belly protruding, I stopped by a tailor. He not only sewed on a new middle button; he secured my top button, too. And he wouldn't accept any money.

I called my credit card company and they removed the ten-dollar fee. I tallied up the day's events: one act of meanness and three acts of kindness. It's the little victories that count. And they clearly outweigh the indignities.

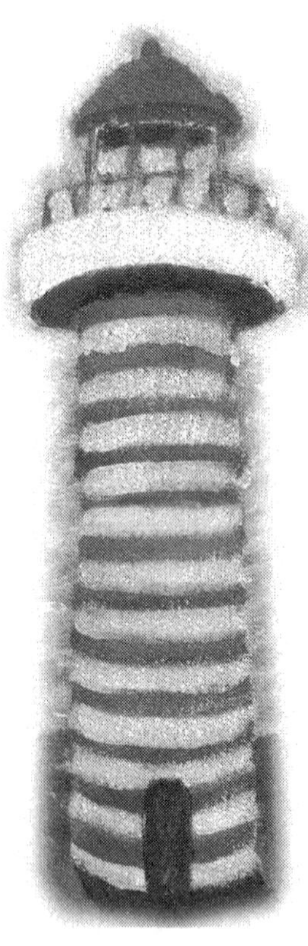

"In this relationship called society, every human being is cutting himself off from another by his position, by his ambition, by his desire for fame, power, and so on; but he has to live in this brutal relationship with other men like himself, so the whole thing is glossed over and made respectable by pleasant-sounding words. In everyday life, each one is devoted to his own interests, though it may be in the name of the country, in the name of peace, or God, and so the isolating process goes on. One becomes aware of this whole process in the form of intense loneliness, a feeling of complete isolation. Thought, which has been giving all importance to itself, isolating itself as the 'me', the ego, has finally come to the point of realizing that it's held in the prison of its own making."

Jiddu Khrishnamurti

The Ups and Downs of the Market

It's Sunday, my favorite day of the week to be in Santa Monica. But I am in Florida, 3,000 miles away. I'm flying back to hang out with friends at the Farmers' Market, my favorite thing to do. I like the easygoing nature of hanging out at the market. It's peaceful, it's free; unlike a party, there's no expectation to be fun or wild. My friends find a table where about ten of us gather. We hang out—so rare these days—away from our computers, phones, and the rush of life. I become ecstatic as time becomes elastic. It trickles by with long gaps between each tick and tock. Live music provides the day's soundtrack. Local farms supply fresh fruit and veggies. Community. Freedom. Nothing planned. No agenda, just spontaneous conversation. It's the one major regret I have about all my traveling: I often miss the Sunday Farmers' Market. But not today! I'm flying back to my favorite place to experience my favorite thing to do.

I wake up at 5 a.m. to catch the first flight out. And I am not a morning person. Morning to me might as well be spelled mourning. But today I spring out of bed before the alarm goes off with a song in my heart; this little piggy is going to market.

At the airport I don't check my bag. I'll scoot off the plane and head right to the market—no waiting at the luggage carousel. The market ends at 1:30. The plane lands at 12:15. I will have an hour at the market. I change planes in Houston and saunter over to my Southwest connection saying good morning to all the beautiful people. I'll get on the plane early because I'm in Group A. This assures that I'll get some bin space. As I stand in line for the second plane, the counter attendant tells me it's a full flight—I'll need to check my bag. She might as well have told me the x-ray machine detected a tumor in my noggin. I say no, I traveled with my bag on the flight here—I want to travel with it on the way home. She shows me the metal bin that bags need to fit into to qualify as carry-on, a space barely big enough to accommodate a lunch box. Mine is too big. I point out that half the bags in line wouldn't fit in that thing. She tells me I need to check my bag. I tell her I can't. She asks why.

"I have a connection," I blurt out, surprising myself. "Where?" She asks.

"Australia."

"When?" she asks skeptically.

I can't think of a time; my brain is empty. I put my head down and mutter, "I don't know."

"You don't know when your plane leaves for Australia?"

I give up. She grabs my bag and puts the white baggage
check label on it like a cop putting on handcuffs. My hour at the market has just been reduced by half. Why didn't I tell her I was rushing back to say my last goodbye to my dad in the hospital? Why didn't I say I had expensive glassware?

Australia? the people waiting in line behind me look at me like I'm carrying explosives. Miss Ticket Counter Killjoy wheels my convicted bag to the front of the plane. There goes my Sunday, my joy. I want to yell, "You've ruined my life, lady!" Then as we board the plane I see my bag still standing there. I steal it back and step into the cabin. A flight attendant notices the white baggage claim ticket and says, "Sir, your bag has been checked. You can't bring that on the plane." I turn and face the disgust-filled eyes of my fellow passengers. Obviously, they have never been to the Sunday Farmers' Market. I put the bag back and slink my sulking, shameful ass back onto the plane. As I sit and stew I see the irony. I was rushing to get to the market because I wanted the experience of having all the time in the world. Why not give myself that sensation now? Happiness doesn't exist outside of me at the Farmers' Market. I create it. It comes from me in any given situation. I can have that slowed down, easy feeling right here, right now, and in every waking moment.

When I get off the flight I use the fifteen minutes waiting for my bag to watch one of my favorite college basketball teams, Temple, play in the NCAA tournament.

I make it to the market before one o'clock, buy some bread, fruit, and flowers, and settle in. About eight of us hang out for the next two hours. I hear the band singing Jimmy Cliff's, "You Can Get It If You Really Want." Yes, with joy as my intention, I can get it. All I need to do is check my baggage.

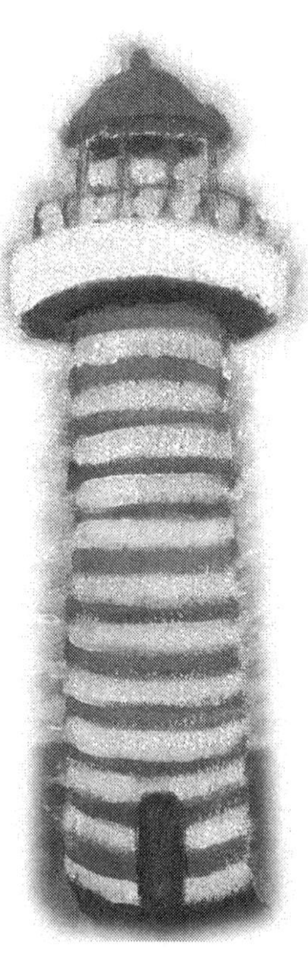

"A bee dancing a map in the air reminds me where a lost day can be found... then I will feel a sudden sting for neglecting the search for what is most sweet."

Tom Hennen

Saturday Night Fiber

It's Saturday night and I'm indulging in a delicious adult beverage—-a raspberry, fiber-rich smoothie. Six raspberries, I've come to learn, contain nine grams of fiber. I've used
twenty-five! What a night this is going to be. Bring it on!

I'm ready to traverse the land spreading apple seeds, avocado seeds, fig seeds, flax seeds. What was once a sluggish metabolism has become a healthy ecosystem. My food now visits like a polite houseguest, never overstaying its welcome.

I had heard people talk about fiber before, but it never registered. Now, by God, it's good golly Miss Broccoli. I was blind, but now I see fiber everywhere. There are whole aisles devoted to fiber in the supermarket, fiber candy bars, fiber cereal. And I've caught the fiber fetish. I want to tell everyone they need more fiber. Cranky woman at the post office: more fiber! How can we control health care costs? More fiber! Want better reception on your iPhone? More fiber optics!

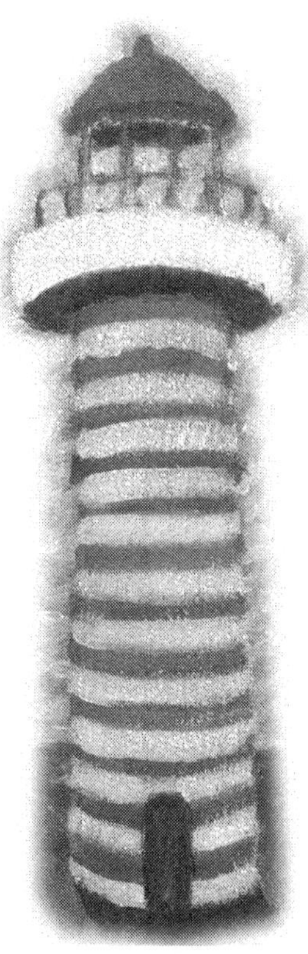

"Exuberance is beauty."
William Blake

Driving Myself Sane

I wanted to get into the left lane, so I put on my blinker. Bad idea. It tipped off the guy a hundred yards behind me. He sped up as if to say, "You're not getting in my lane, pal. You're not getting one car length ahead of me and ruining my life." I wanted to get even, get in front of him and slam on my brakes. I sped up. He sped up. I sped up. He sped up. I looked at my speedometer. I was going 96 miles an hour. I thought, "Paul, settle down. This is a Ford Escort. What are you doing? How did you get sucked into this guy's misery?"

Why can't I slow down? Why am I so quickly upset? What am I running from or to? When I die, no matter how much I've done, there will be plenty I didn't accomplish. What's most important is did I enjoy the ride? I always say that; I always forget it. Why should I let little things bother me? Someday I'll be dead. Some guy's blocking my lane? Big deal, someday he'll be dead too. Ha!

My life has been like the movie, *Groundhog's Day*. Every day while I'm driving someone cuts me off; why do I continue to get upset every time? Why not accept it? Enjoy it. "Oh, there you are, Mister in a Big Fat Hurry—I expected you twenty minutes ago. You had me worried."

How worthwhile is any accomplishment if it's done without joy? Isn't the quality of my life more important than all the things I stuff it with? No need to think in terms of minutes; I want to create as many quality moments each day as I can.

Modern life would have us believe achievement is what's most important. Our own sense of wonder and awe at the world we get to live in takes a back seat. I notice the glee my dog takes in the car, his face out the window, his tongue wagging. He's thinking, "Oh my God! I'm going sixty miles per hour. I'm not even moving my legs.
Wow! Bow wow!"

Can I handle this? Yes, I can. What I need is my own intention to be the happiest driver on the road. Carpe diem mañana. Slow down. Seize joy! So now, when I want to get into the left lane, I put on my right blinker.

As I got ready to publish this book I got obsessed with having it published by my dad's 85th birthday. As the date loomed closer I panicked. To keep writing I began drinking lots of coffee, sodas, and smoking cigars. I realized

I can be with my dad on his 85th birthday

and that is the greatest gift I can give him. I gave my deadline a lifeline. It would be done when I loved it. It is so easy to get caught up in ambition and to forget that the reason for being is joy.

Ahhhh...

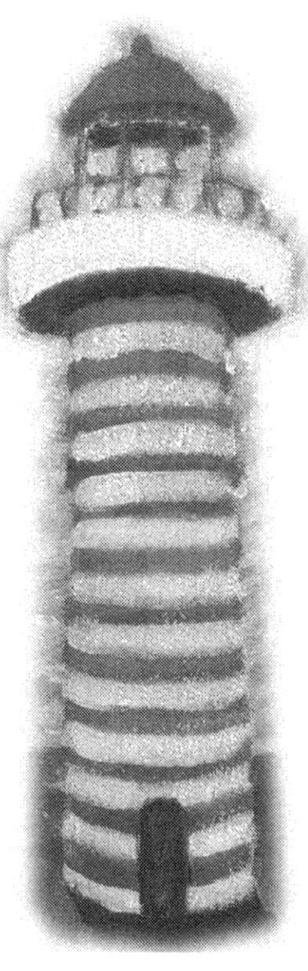

"One of the greatest stumbling blocks in life is this constant struggle to reach, to achieve, to acquire. We are trained from childhood to acquire and to achieve - the very brain cells themselves create and demand this pattern of achievement in order to have physical security, but psychological security is not within the field of achievement."

Jiddu Krisnamurti

Amazing Grace

Thanks to Facebook, I got reacquainted with my old friend, Star. I first met him twenty years ago when he was living on the streets in New York City. He earned an honest living on Astor Street, selling objects that had been discarded. He was a sober, well-dressed, soft-spoken and smart twenty- eight-year-old African-American. "Paul," he once said, "you wouldn't believe what people throw away." Everything he was wearing had been thrown out, including his perfectly fitted designer jeans. I picked out two art deco lamps displayed on his blanket, then realized I had no money. Star gave them to me.

Star was sleeping in Tompkins Square Park, some nights through pelting sleet and snow. Two years earlier, he had come home and found his wife with another man. He moved out and could no longer focus at work, so he lost his janitorial foreman's job. When Star was three, his alcoholic father abandoned the family. "I promised myself I would never do that to my kids, Paul, and here I went and did it."

I spent some free time over the next four years helping him get off the streets. With the help of some friends, I got him work and took him back to see his kids. It was the most wonderful experience of my life. It was as if I was helping myself.

I saw so much of myself in Star. I still harbored resentments from my own childhood over my dad, or who I had made him out to be. I was still holding onto something my dad yelled at me years ago: "Wake up, you'll never amount to anything." I was also weighed down with guilt for leaving my own child, by giving him up for adoption when I was seventeen.

Star found work and a place to live for six months, but quit because his boss kept belittling him. He wound up back on the streets. Star then painted houses with my brother for a while until the work dried up. He again wound up back on the streets. When I was out of town a few times each month, Star stayed in my apartment. I came back once to find some possessions gone. Star had succumbed to heroin. I had no anger about him taking my things, which surprised me.

Maybe I had a lesson to learn about boundaries, but I knew Star was a remarkable man who was lost. Humiliated, he apologized profusely. I accepted his apology; our friendship was more important to me than my possessions.

When I met Star, all my energy had been going into my stand-up comedy career. I was so afraid of not getting what I needed: to be famous, to prove myself, to pay rent. I had no time for a balanced life that included vacations, relationships, or sunsets. Being with Star opened my heart. I knew he would prevail. As the mystic Osho said: "When we love, we are the first to benefit."

Five years after meeting Star, I moved to Los Angeles, where my career seriously faltered. I was thirty-seven, at the lowest point in my life. I went bankrupt, felt bankrupt. Then Star called. He was now a building manager in Brooklyn, finishing college, back in his sons' lives, and sober for four years. And he told me, "I can't thank you enough for all you've done for me, Paul."

I welled up with tears. If he'd prevailed, so could I. I wanted to make a living doing something that gave me the same feeling I had while being with Star. So I went into teaching. Quitting stand-up was humiliating, but it was a blow to my ego, not my heart.

I was humbled. I saw my dad in a new light. I was embarrassed all those years because my dad drove a ten-year-old car and because he was a mailman and a janitor. He lived within his means to give us the best life possible. Now, I see that Dad has always been fighting for me, even as I was fighting against him. When we are young, we project our fears onto the person who brings them up in us. The filter through which I looked out into the world affirmed my core belief: I don't belong. This world doesn't support who I am. But that notion began to shift. I started to hear the words my dad had said in a different light. He was right—I wouldn't amount to anything if I didn't wake up, if I didn't become aware of how my mind was sabotaging me. I was doomed if I continued to live with my current mindset. Someone once complimented my shirt, and I thought, "What's wrong with my pants?" My world was dark because I kept turning off the light.

Star went blind four years ago. His doctors don't know what caused it. His upbeat attitude amazed me. "Paul, not once have I asked, Why me?'" he said. "Aside from the initial shock and fear, I'm in a new place of gratitude, and oddly enough, I have a vision I never had."

Every time something is lost, something is gained. "Paul, as a child my biggest fear was the dark. Can you believe that? Now I get around on my own, cross the street on my own. Sometimes I get help, but I can do more than I ever thought. I do my own laundry, cook my own meals. I have a new awareness. I know where every single item in my apartment is. While I was in my blind rehab, a man took us out on walks, pointed out where the coffee shops were, the hot dog stands and the banks. He did this every day for two weeks. I later found out he was totally blind himself. Can you believe it? Paul, that's when I knew I could handle this. I have my children in my life. I even talked to my dad before he died. He sobered up, reunited with my mom, and fell off the wagon—but he died sober. I have survived so much. My mom raised seven kids. I could see the dirt through the floorboards in our kitchen. Get this, we had no stove—my mom would make French toast with an iron. Paul, all of that prepared me to handle this. My family helps me; my friends do, too. I am blessed."

I saw myself in Star, and I now want to see myself in everyone. Just when I was getting too caught up in my career and money, Star reminded me what it's all about. Being. Being grateful. Getting in touch with the vision behind our seeing, the vision that we came into this life with, the vision that lives on.

I realized what Star had given me: he let me help him. I am considering buying a house, and my dad once again wants to help me.

For years I wanted my dad to apologize, never realizing all the good things he repeatedly has done for me and for always looking past the chip on my shoulder to continue to help me. Pop has always been there for me. I see how blessed I was to have two incredibly supportive and loving parents. It's never too late to have a great childhood.

I see the grunt work love requires. I see the concern my father's offer represents. I see how easy it is to hurt someone. How devastating it is to have your love unaccepted. I know how hard it is to say I'm sorry. I've yet to tell him, but I've accepted my dad's help and our faltering, expanding hearts.

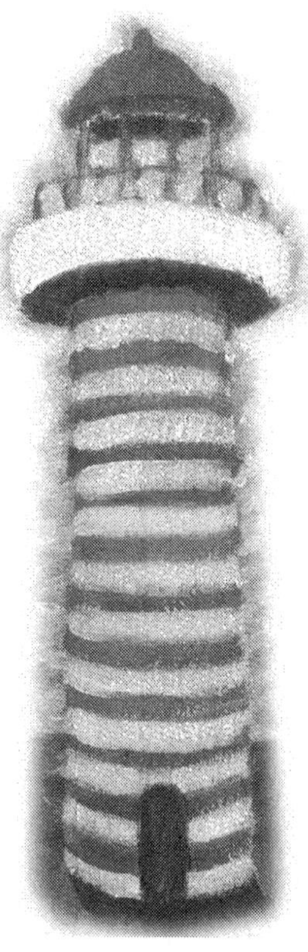

"One's destination is never a place but a new way of seeing things."

Henry Miller

My Apologies

After reading the last chapter, "Amazing Grace," my good friend Laurence asked me why I had yet to apologize to my father. I find it easy to apologize to most people. I pride myself on it. In fact, years ago when I was teaching, my seventh grade students got sick of me apologizing to them for having lost my temper. I never understood why they would tell me there was no need to apologize. Maybe they thought it was appropriate to lose one's temper when students throw things at you.

I have always seen anger as wrong. Period. It was while teaching and experiencing a classroom of energy-crazed, pubescent adolescents that I finally understood what it was like for my dad to be dealing with seven sons. The students taught me that my anger wasn't a mistake, it was part of the passion of wanting to make a difference in their lives. In his commitment to me, Pop risked being enraged and disliked. I was out to be better than Pop; he was out to make me better. Underneath his temper was an intense concern for what he thought was best for me. Usually, we all have the best intentions, just not the right delivery.

Why was it so hard for me to apologize to him? It wasn't so much that I'd be apologizing: I'd be changing who I was. When I apologized to the class I was honoring my ideal of never losing my temper. But apologizing to my dad would mean letting go of who I'd been. It would mean letting go of what made me better than my dad. It would mean seeing myself for the jerk I could be. It would change me.

The next time I had breakfast with Pop I told him that as I wrote this book I was seeing just how much he'd supported me, how generous he'd been with his time, with his money, with his encouragement. I was sorry that he had to deal with the chip on my shoulder. He said I didn't have to apologize for anything. He had no resentment toward me at all.

I found myself getting choked up as I told him it meant a lot to me after he saw my first stand up comedy performance and said he was never prouder in his life. For the first time, thirty years after he said it, I heard what he had said, I let it in. It moved me. And I saw past the slights I kept collecting to realize that this man, a stranger to me for so many years, was my biggest ally. All my years of making something of myself, of proving myself, were unnecessary. But they served their purpose in getting me to this point, to the truth. My dad was never against me; the world has not been against me. For so long I was a stranger to myself. Wanting to fix what was unbroken. A narcissist wanting to be some one else. A self righteous know-it-all with an inferiority complex.

I looked up at my dad. The man whose features I have inherited: his strong nose, his pale pink skin, his blue eyes and more recently his white hair. Even our smiles matched as we glanced at each other, the right sides rising higher to form a smirk. And I said, "Well, there is something I do have to say." And as tears welled up I said, "Thank you." And then we both uttered the same question, "Wanna watch the Phillies game?"

Today, missing my hair...

...I combed the beach.

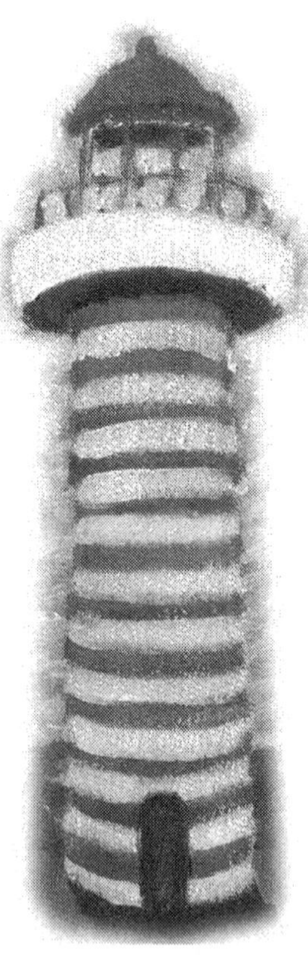

"Conflict can exist only so long as there is reaction to that environment which produces the "I", the self. The majority of people are unconscious of this conflict - the conflict between one's self, which is but the result of the environment, and the environment itself; very few are conscious of this continuous battle. One becomes conscious of that conflict, that disharmony, that struggle between the false creation of the environment, which is the "I", and the environment itself, only through suffering."

Juddu Krishnamurti

The Happy Ending

I fell in love a year and a half ago with Emma, who lives "carpe diem mañana." Her days are not weighed down with things to do but open to things to spontaneously enjoy. She will do anything that brings a smile. She will also cry in awe at a sunset. I, on the other hand, see sunsets as bad news— the day is over and I've barely gotten anything done. I have no check marks on my to-do list. Damn you, majestic purple marbled sky!

Over these last eighteen months I've taken more time off, slowed down, and smiled more than ever before. I now trust that the universe is providing everything I need. By seizing the day tomorrow I am able to see that real joy comes from the serendipities of an open, trusting heart. It's about seeing the day with open eyes, not seizing it with blinders on; taking life in, not taking it over.

Thanks to my relationship with Emma I see myself more clearly. How quick I am to play the victim. After four months in our relationship I was still paying for every single dinner. I then realized I'd set myself up for this slight by needing to be seen as a generous guy. Emma had offered to pay a few times and I rejected her offer, hoping, of course, she would absolutely insist. But she didn't. Once I mentioned what was bothering me she understood completely. She simply thought paying the bill made me smile. Nope. That's another lesson I've learned: I'm cheap.

It's been an incredible relationship and it's heartbreaking that it's ending. My career has me out of town about every other week. Emma tends to close down a little a day before I leave and takes a day to warm up when I come home again. I always wished my leaving would cause her to kiss me like a soldier going off to war—and that upon my return she'd kiss me like a decorated hero. When I shared this with her she said jokingly but wistfully, "I want the war to be over."

Over the last year I had cut back significantly on my traveling and it bothered me. And the traveling I was still doing bothered Emma. Our spirits were dampened and we had to acknowledge the truth: we were losing ourselves in the relationship, forcing ourselves into clothes that didn't fit.

We had the most loving breakup, and celebrated the wonderful highlights: the two of us crashing a wedding on our third date, dancing and getting applause from the guests; Emma hopping into a handicapped grocery cart and me wheeling her around the supermarket; our month long trek in Nepal where we got to share our love of nature and the simple life with people who greet each other with "namaste"—and mean it.

I thought the time we spent in Nepal would ease my ten days away when we got back. But it was even harder on her. And her disappointment was very hard on me. I wouldn't change a thing; I wouldn't have wanted it to end a minute sooner. Each time we came to a point that looked like it might be the end a talk brought us to a deeper connection. Later, I would look back and think I'm so glad we didn't end it then because of how I got to experience us afterward. There was always more to Emma than I realized, and more to me.

But ultimately our talks led us to face our fundamental differences. For Emma, lots of proximity builds desire and connection; for me a certain amount of distance builds excitement and connection. If we held on it would have been out of dependency and fear, not love.

The romance was remarkable and losing it is very sad. I am grateful and grieving. It hurts, but that doesn't mean we're making a mistake. I feel so lucky to have experienced us. There's no longer us but I still have Emma as a true friend. Our love wants nothing more than to give each other wings. She allows me the space to be absolutely honest, silly, and still. I now trust myself and others so much more. I feel taller. I experienced eighteen months of being loved and loving, and now I'm in a place where I'm not dependent on being loved. There's no notion of either of us being right or wrong. Life is three-dimensional, with the truth living in its depths.

I look back on our breakup and feel the way I did after each talk we had; it led us to the perfect place.

Communication cleared up what was stifling us, though it couldn't alter our differences. I'm glad we didn't hold on this time. We let go. We are better equipped than ever to fly. A relationship can end and be divine. Some moments bring memories that make me wilt; some moments let me see how much I've grown and I thrive.

I will fall in love with being alone; I will fall in love again, knowing more clearly what I want in a relationship. I've expanded my work on the road and I love it. Emma taught me the joy of letting the day surprise me. I now watch the sunsets and relish them. I love life. I'm taking people in. I'm more open than ever. I do what makes me smile and think of Emma. Someone once said that the sign of a sophisticated mind is being able to hold two opposing views simultaneously; I believe maturity is being able to hold two opposing feelings simultaneously. Where I find myself is fascinating and frightening. This experience is very sad. And perfectly wonderful.

When I tell friends about the breakup their response is "sorry." I understand and appreciate that, but they might also add, "and congratulations."

The Family Vacation and Other Oxymorons

It's the first day of our family vacation. Dad and all seven sons have rented an oceanfront house. I comb the beach with a few of my brothers: Bill, Chris, and John. I'm feeling cool, wearing my favorite shirt from CBGB's, ready to let go of work and reap the rewards of a life well lived.

My brother Bill asks, "What's new?"

"Well, I just finished my book." "What's it called?" asks Chris.

"Carpe Diem, Mañana."

"What's that mean?" asks John.

"Seize the day, tomorrow."

"That doesn't even make sense," Bill says. "Paul, I'm in marketing. People want to buy a book that makes them feel warm and fuzzy."

I say, "How about Carpe Cockapoo?"

"How many pages is it?" asks Chris.

"About two hundred."

Bill says, "Two hundred? Who wants to read a book that's two hundred pages?"

"I think it's been done, Bill. Why? Are you still reading *The Hungry Caterpillar*?"

Chris asks, "What kind of book is it?"

"Humor and philosophy."

John says, "No one reads philosophy."

"Paul, no one is going to buy a philosophy book that's two hundred pages with a title in Spanish," says Bill, the marketing genius who is currently on my calling plan because of his anemic credit score.

"Carpe diem is Latin. Manaña is Spanish."

Bill gets animated: "How are they going to know the book's in English? People make up their minds in ten seconds. Paul, you have to grab people right away."

"There are laws against that, Bill."

"So, what is your philosophy?" asks John.

"It's about living from your heart, not your head; seeking joy, not results."

Chris shouts over the pounding waves, "It take two hundred pages to say that?"

"Why don't you do a survey and ask people if they like the title?" Bill asks.

"Because I love the title, Bill. I wrote this book for me. I don't want to spend an ounce of time figuring out what other people might like. I'm going to give you guys one piece of unsolicited advice: stop giving unsolicited advice." As I say this a woman walks by and compliments my shirt.

Bill asks, "What's your shirt say?" I tell him, "Carpe diem, mañana."

We all laugh. John asks, "How much are you selling the book for?"

"Twenty bucks."

"Why not make it two books and sell them for ten bucks each," Bill says, demonstrating why his skills pay some of the bills.

"I might," I say, "or maybe I'll sell it by the page."

"How many hours have you spent working on it?" Chris asks.

"I have no idea. All I know is I've loved every minute of it."

I didn't expect this onslaught, but for the first time I don't feel belittled, just amused. If Jesus were in my family he would have stuck with carpentry.

My six brothers and I are back to celebrate Dad's eighty- fifth birthday. And this is how we celebrate. In my family even a walk on the beach is no walk on the beach. This is our first family reunion at the Jersey shore since Mom died eight years ago. Before she died we spent a week at the beach every summer for forty-five years.

The glut of testosterone in my family is overwhelming. That's why Mom was so important to all of us. When I was four years old playing with matches my pant leg caught fire sending me to the hospital for three months. Every afternoon I had Mom all to myself for two hours. I didn't want it to be over. The day I got out of the hospital I was caught playing with matches again.

My family tends to be both extremely sensitive and extremely insensitive. Tim, the youngest, put a gargantuan effort into getting this reunion together. He wrote out long lists of things to bring and do. He spent hours filling up his SUV with tents, volleyball equipment, bikes, boogie boards, a poker table, food, a keg, etc. It was so full no one else could fit in the car with him. His enthusiasm morphed into anxiety.

I had offered to make Mom's coleslaw but made the first batch with what I had available, so it was Stevia instead of sugar and Trader Joe's mayo instead of Hellman's. I told Tim I would go to the Acme later and buy the exact ingredients Mom used for the next bowl. He exploded. "Jesus! Damn it, Paul! Why couldn't you have done that first? All you think about is yourself. Why couldn't you make Mom's coleslaw. That's such a suck-ass thing to do. It's all about you, all the fricking time." I was taken aback. In the past I would have remained quiet and convinced myself I was above all this. This time I had to defend myself.

"Tim, just because you put a lot of time into this family reunion doesn't mean you can be an asshole. Chill out. I will make Mom's coleslaw." "Oh, grow up!" he shouted as he stomped out.

I went to the beach and played with my nieces and nephews. When I came back I ran into Tim. "I'm sorry," he said. "It's just that I'm really missing Mom right now. I was just crying for a half hour. I miss her so much. I'm so sorry I wasn't there for her at the end. I couldn't stand seeing her in the nursing home like that. I let her down."

We hug. I say, "Tim, Mom never saw it that way. With Mom we could do no wrong -- she loved us all as we are. Every single one of us felt so big in her eyes. Let's honor her this week and see each other through her eyes." Tim nods and wipes a tear away. "Yeah, I love you, man." And I say, "Oh, grow up."

Vacation over, I head back to "work." Carnival Cruise Lines flies me to Amsterdam. I have just gotten a raise. Life is good.

And I am finding that people are the same wherever you go. In Amsterdam I ride my bike behind an 85 year old woman. She signals with her left arm as she turns, and keeps her arm out for the next 30 minutes...

Eat, Pray, Louvre

Paris, the City of Love; for this past week I couldn't keep my hands off me. Being alone in Paris allows me to have her romantic beauty all to myself. In Amsterdam I was thinking about Emma all week. For the eight months before this trip we'd gotten along so well. Perhaps because we'd broken up. I asked her to meet me in Paris. She said she was in love with someone else, the love of her life. I took that as a no.

The first few days I woke up feeling lonely. I was on vacation but felt nothing but self-pity. I couldn't even enjoy myself in Amsterdam -- who was going to love me? I told myself these next two weeks would be my spiritual journey. Whatever came along would be perfect, would help me with my healing. And I could let go of Emma. As Maya Angelou says, "Letting go isn't painful; holding on is." Luckily, nothing makes you want to let go and sing "la da dee, la de dah" like riding a bike through Amsterdam -- the open sky, the unique boutiques, coffee cafes, and furniture stores. And above these mom and pop shops, nestled inside the ancient, finely detailed architecture, were apartments. How wonderful to be able to say, "Honey, I'm going downstairs for a latte and an ottoman." It seems everyone in Amsterdam owned a bike and a shop selling things they loved; each store had its own personality. I stayed in an apartment I rented through Airbnb for fifty-five dollars a night on a lonely street that could have been in Queens, New York. But this is the sidewalk on which I found myself skipping in the rain. I had asked a waiter where I could buy a cheap umbrella and he gave me one from the lost and found.

I went to the Van Gogh Museum twice, totally moved by the resplendent, vibrating scenes of nature unable to contain her bursting beauty. I sailed through the canals and strolled through the tree-lined neighborhoods. Even loved hearing the emergency sirens; their melody reminded me of bagpipes. And I didn't even know I cared for bagpipes.

I met a local artist who found the courage to open her own shop when she asked herself, "If you're not sure of yourelf, who is?"

On my last day in Amsterdam I strolled through the voluminous and densely wooded Vondelpark. The sun was setting in shades of pink and tangerine as I breathed in the same air as Vincent. Clouds drifting by, wisps of whimsy parading their quirky shapes, reflecting the sun in peacock-colored puffs, clumps, and clusters. What a way for the day to end.

Every cloud is a silver lining!

Dusk had become a starry, starry night by the time I got back to my street. On this, my last night, I knew I would miss this street so much, which struck me as odd. All week this block was drab; what gave it special meaning now? Then I understood: endings are what show us life's significance. Parting has a way of showing us what's essential about a place, a life, a relationship. Eulogies don't harp on a dead man's foibles. What matters is what touched our heart. I want to live knowing that I will die, that anything I accomplish will end; by knowing that, I can let go of anything that doesn't really matter, that doesn't touch the heart.

I could appreciate where my relationship with Emma had brought me, what it had awakened in me. I was filled with happiness for her and for her new relationship. I was thrilled that we had found a way to love each other. Thanks to this street, Amsterdam will always be a part of me. If you miss something that's become a part of you, you are looking at it the wrong way.

And now I'm approaching the end of my week in Paris. I lollygag along the Seine and think, "Wow, I am lollygagging along the Seine!" I shuffle toward the Eiffel tower; the full moon has my back. I catch a glimpse of the top of her steepled hat, then she disappears behind the tall buildings only to reappear between other buildings revealing even more of her iconic body, then disappears again, reappearing finally in her full, flowing iron gown.

Today I am content seeing her from a distance. No longer needing any more experiences, any more must-do's, I sit beside a willow tree, its branches cascading down, housing me in a verdant snow globe across from the Louvre, which I never entered. And I don't care; I did everything that Paris called me to do, sauntering all over and relishing it all: the shops, the Museum d'Orsay, the artists at Montmartre, Notre Dame, Shakespeare and Company, the cafes, and the green bins overflowing with books and posters along the Seine.

As the branches envelop me and the river reflects the moon, I recall that Simone Weil once said, "Attention is the purest form of generosity." Life is about cherishing these little moments. And there are no little moments when we take life in.

It wasn't a visit to the Louvre that taught me this; it was a whisper from a willow.

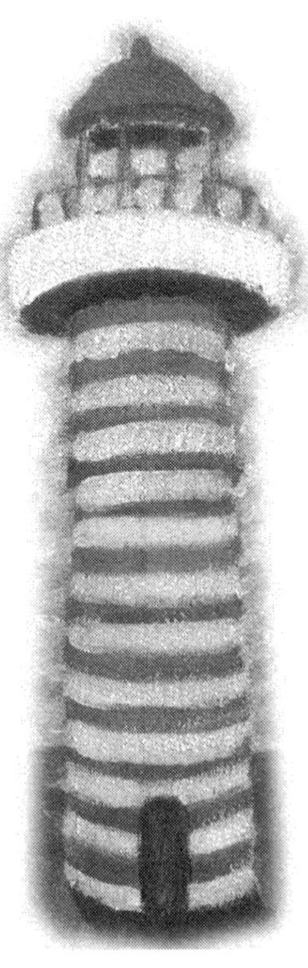

"You see things and say, 'Why?'
But I dream things that never
were; and I say, 'Why not?'"
George Bernard Shaw

Why Not?

I wrote Carpe Diem, Mañana because I dreamed of a life I had yet to live. Before I started writing it, I had been caught up in what I thought was seizing the day. My career in stand-up comedy had brought me to many beautiful cities; but when people asked me about them, I realized all I'd experienced was the Holiday Inn. My days had been spent working in my room. I thought I was getting ahead, but in truth life was passing me by. I decided that I wanted to let my joy and spirit seize the day, not my ego and agenda. Success would then come from the amount of joy I collected. Living would be my writing, my work. Learning to enjoy each moment would prepare me for every moment that followed. Every day would be a blank canvas. Instead of knowing how the day will unfold, I'd let questions guide me. Can I rise and really shine—shine the way children shine? Can I shine even though I 'm not at the perfect weight, the perfect place, or the perfect income? Despite my flaws, can I be whole and complete? With wounds still open, can my heart be open, too? Why not?

I began writing this book as I was turning fifty and feeling old. And three years later, I realize I was young. I could remember names. I could bend over. When I was done peeing, I was done peeing. It's a wonderful paradox that as life gets harder I'm enjoying it more.

I no longer try to fit into the world. I let the world fit into me. I know I belong here. I don't have to amount to anything. I can be nothing and know I have it all. I am here to experience joy, honesty, and compassion. I am beginning to understand there is good news to be discovered in everything. Nobody cares? Then can I skip down the street and sing to my heart's delight.

Why not? The end of dignity is the beginning of freedom. I often find myself losing patience, losing my temper, and getting attached to a daily agenda. I have learned to quickly get back to joy. Experiencing this moment is more important than anything I wanted to accomplish. As John Lennon sings: "Life is what happens to you while you're busy making other plans."

This book is a measure of my spiritual success. I will keep asking myself questions. How often do I smile? Do I take others in? How often am I kind? Am I gentle to myself? How often do I catch myself getting upset and regain my peace of mind? How often do I admit being wrong? Do I see the joy in pain and sorrow as they lead me to the truth? How often do I acknowledge what I am grateful for? How often do I challenge the voices that bring me down? How often do I listen to the thoughts that build me up?

In my spiritual practice I use affirmations and post them all around my house. But I need to remember to take these notes down when I have guests over. During a party a friend walked out of my bathroom and said,

"Paul, your candle went out but luckily your smile lights up a room."

Can I see failures as a steady procession toward success? Can I see fears as illusions to outgrow? Can I delight myself with what I am willing to do? Can I show up and shine with- out effort, like the sun? Why not?

My mom died seven years ago, yet she still receives coupons in the mail. Now I know what they mean by Bed, Bath, and Beyond. Her death freed me from the fear death had over me. My spirit will live on. But while I'm here, I want to shine. Can I appreciate the wisdom of all I've been through? Can I realize that I've never been better, more experienced, more tolerant, and more understanding than I am right now? I know that life doesn't always give me what I want, but always gives me who I am? Why not?

I have witnessed my dad shift from obsessing over death to accepting death. Another paradox I've taken to heart is that we can't fully live until we've accepted death. Despite the fragility that comes with age, Pop lives with grace and humor. I'd taken him to the doctor's office for a physical, and the nurse asked, "Mr. Lyons, you need to change into a robe; do you wear boxers or briefs?" My dad smirked and said, "Depends." Can I be happy for no reason at all? Instead of taking life over, can I take life in? Amidst doubt and uncertainty, can I shine? Amidst breakups and breakdowns, can I shine? Without anyone's approval, can I shine? Can I design a life that is totally mine? Why not?

Single, I went back to internet dating. I don't see how it works for so many people. This one woman wrote in her profile that she loved the great outdoors and she did. She was homeless.

So that only lasted six months.

At first it was a lot of fun. We'd go for walks in the park and I could leave her there.

This other woman failed to include some pertinent information in her profile. I found out on the first date, she had three DUI's, two restraining orders, and a penis.

So that only lasted six months.

Well, we had something in common.

A Life Worth Eavesdropping On

Jane wasn't wearing lipstick. Maybe this wasn't a date. We had reconnected on Facebook. I messaged her that my ship would be in New York City. She responded, "I'm right at the docks, baby." From that one line I recalled her passion, her sensuality, her playfulness.

We couldn't remember why we stopped dating 25 years ago. Sitting at an outdoor café by the docks she said, "Well, back then I was just divorced, had a baby, no parents. I was a mess." I said, "Yes, I was just divorced and scared, too." Then I added, "It's not like I'm not a mess now, I'm just willing to be seen." We both smiled. Jane put on lipstick.

We talked about how, since our divorces, we'd both had safe relationships. Every one I'd been in had an exit strategy, always with one foot out, which allowed me not to be honest. Whenever I got disappointed I rarely spoke up thinking I would be moving on anyway. Jane said her safety was dating much younger men. At 53, though she couldn't call herself a cougar, she was a Mellencamp.

"Every relationship requires a certain tension," Jane said. In one word she summed up what had been missing in my last relationship- a healthy tension. All of life requires tension and release. Music is tension and release. Sex is tension and release. Jokes are tension and release. With conflict there's growth, as long as you resolve it with communication and honesty.

I went to the bathroom. When I got back, the women sitting at the table next to us said, "Sorry, I couldn't help eavesdropping on your conversation. You know what I'm thinking? When Harry Met Sally."

And Jane said, "Well, I haven't had the orgasm yet."

The woman, laughing added, "I'll have what she is having."

Wow, I have a life worth eavesdropping on. All the lessons learned, all the fears overcome, everything that has brought me to this incredible place, a life with more understanding and joy than ever before. When I was younger I compared myself to others whose lives seemed so charmed. Now I see that everyone grows up confused, everybody suffers. Once we accept that life is difficult it suddenly gets easier. And now I compare myself to my younger, insecure self and enjoy who I have become. I find myself ready for a relationship with integrity and commitment.

Jane and I walked to the ship and said good-bye. I hugged her, longing to kiss her.

For the next two weeks we talked, texted, Facebooked, emailed, and fell for each other. I flew back to New York to spend five days with her. On our last day she wanted to picnic in Central Park. I mentioned making love there. Jane joked, "The police would never believe it was consensual."

Hearing about my brothers, Jane asked, "Seven boys? And no one is gay?"

I said, "Well, I come the closest." She laughed and I told her, "I have had some homosexual experiences." I haven't been open about that before, feeling that it would turn a woman off.

She said, "Wow, you are even more interesting than I thought." Amazing, I never looked at it that way- those explorations gave me more depth, more character.

Our first night sleeping together in a hotel room opened my eyes to what's possible. I had many fantasies about what we would do, however, I developed a high fever. Jane stopped and got a towel and wiped my forehead. Then she began a sneezing jag. As she wiped my forehead her running nose dripped onto my face. She winced, "Oh, that's real sexy." We laughed. I never felt so loved. You know you have life licked when you can appreciate what happens even more than what you wanted to happen.

Who knows where this will lead? I know I am committed to it working, thriving. And I know for the first time in my life I'm in a relationship where I have both feet in. And most importantly, my heart.

About the Author

"... a deviously creative funnyman."
—The Rocky Mountain News.

"Hysterical."
—Stephen Wright

"His comedy is wonderfully wholesome and significantly different."
—Silver Freedman, owner of the original Improvisation.

Paul Lyons presents his inspirational comedy everywhere: clubs, corporate events, cruise ships, and wherever two or more are gathered in his name. His many TV appearances include acting and stand-up performances on Comedy Central, CBS, and Showtime. Paul has headlined throughout the United States, as well as in London and Australia. His essays have been published in *Details* magazine, *TV Guide*, and *Playgirl*.

Paul hates to brag, but he has over sixty friends on Facebook and nearly a dozen Twitter followers. As a personal life coach, his clients include Charlie Sheen, Lindsay Lohan, and Honey BooBoo.

His weekly blog can be found at Laughlyons.com and on Facebook.

Email: Pawlyons@gmail.com

Special Thanks

Thanks to Christy Walker for guiding me through the first edition of this book as well as newer essays in this edition. A joy to work with, her editorial expertise helped transform my words into clear, humorous, and honest essays.

Thanks to Jackie and Jonathan at Selfpublishing.com for making this whole process joyful and seamless with their insights and design.

Thanks to Dan Marcus whose dedication helped shape and bring this book to life. Dan has an impeccable eye for story, style, humor, and truth.

And thanks to artist Rod Boston for the cover design, his art is a great example of the beauty that's possible when we follow our heart.

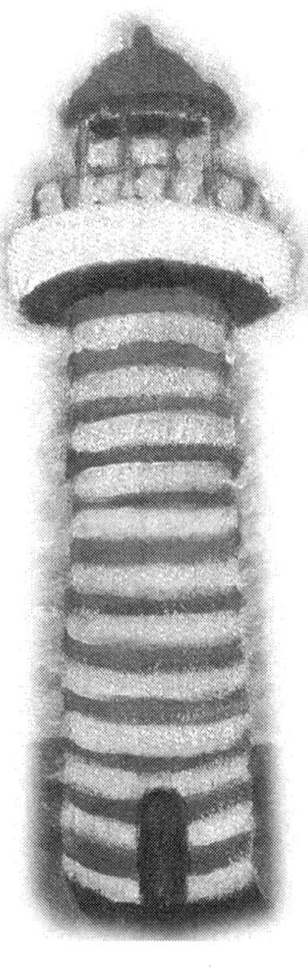

"When you let go it all gets done; when you try and try the world is beyond winning."

Lao Tzu (604-532 B.C.)

Made in the USA
Middletown, DE
12 January 2018